THE HOLY INNOCENTS
AND OTHER POEMS

THE MYSTERY OF
THE HOLY INNOCENTS

AND OTHER POEMS

BY

CHARLES PEGUY

Translated by
PANSY PAKENHAM

With an Introduction by
ALEXANDER DRU

WIPF & STOCK · Eugene, Oregon

Wipf and Stock Publishers
199 W 8th Ave, Suite 3
Eugene, OR 97401

The Mystery of the Holy Innocents and Other Poems
By Péguy, Charles and Pakenham, Pansy
ISBN 13: 978-1-5326-4585-3
Publication date 12/13/2017
Previously published by The Harvill Press Ltd., 1956

CONTENTS

INTRODUCTION

CHARLES PEGUY is the only poet of consequence during the last fifty years in France whose work has failed to arouse the smallest critical interest in this country. Compared with Claudel or Valéry, to mention two of his contemporaries, he has simply fallen flat. It almost seems as though the term 'poetry' were out of place, or as though, and this is perhaps nearer the truth, the conception of poetry his work implied placed it outside the pale of contemporary criticism. There seems to be nothing for criticism to get its teeth into. Everything is plain sailing. There is no shell to crack, no secret to explore, no difficulty of language, no impenetrable thought, no interplay of images to be unravelled. In whatever direction the critic looks, whether at the technique, the ideas, the images or the psychological sphere, there is nothing to be done, or at any rate nothing worth doing.

But in addition to this negative quality, which disqualifies Péguy at the start, there are some very palpable positive elements in his work which seem to settle the matter for good and all. He is not merely eccentric, in the sense of being outside the French literary tradition; he is all too easy to label. There can be no doubt where he belongs, with his Mysteries, his Tapestries, his saints and his pilgrimages. The atmosphere is all too familiar: the deliberately archaic world of a stylised, mediaeval Catholicism, the refuge of the convert in reaction against the modern world, returning in his poetry to the true fold of the past.

INTRODUCTION

The Mystery of the Holy Innocents and the selections from his other poetic works collected in this volume are, like all his work, perfectly straightforward and do not call for comment. But it may not be out of place to try and forestall some of the misunderstandings which cluster round his work, and to suggest where the critical problem lies, not for the sake of raising a question, but in order to clear the way for a fuller understanding of the poetry itself. For whether Péguy's poetry is ultimately judged to have failed or succeeded, whether he is recognised as an important writer or not, there is no doubt whatever that it remains of the greatest interest and implies a conception of poetry and of the function of the imagination which, as I shall suggest, illustrates the truth of Coleridge's notion of poetry, more distinctly in certain respects, than Wordsworth himself. This does not of course imply any comparison between the merits of Péguy and Wordsworth, and in general I have no intention in what follows of awarding marks to Péguy, but of explaining quite briefly what Péguy thought he was doing. Nor shall I deal specifically with the poems in this volume, which can only be done at greater length and in detail.

Péguy's poetry grew straight out of his prose and it is even possible to point to the pages in *St. Joan* where his prose smoulders, catches fire and bursts into flame. With the exception of some lines of doggerel in the first version of *St. Joan* * Péguy wrote no poetry, and did not think of writing poetry, until he was thirty-five, six years before his death in 1914. His poetry, he said, was prepared by twenty years of prose, or more accurately by about twenty volumes of prose. Then, in 1908 he informed Joseph Lotte that he had 're-become' a Catholic, and shortly afterwards he told

* *Jeanne d'Arc*, 1898.

Daniel Halévy, that he had begun writing poetry. Of the
two men, Halévy was the more surprised and, one might
safely add, the more incredulous.

The metamorphosis which took place in Péguy at this
period was a double event: his return to Catholicism and
the release of his imagination, the birth of his poetry, are
two facets of the same spiritual renewal, and the character
of his poetry cannot be understood apart from its source;
so that before turning to his poetry it is necessary to say
two words about his return to Catholicism. In the first
place, it is important to observe that Péguy would never
allow that he was a 'convert'. Morally, spiritually, intellec-
tually, he had nothing to disavow except his sins. He was
not converted *from* anything. He continued to hold the same
views, and his criticism of Catholicism was sharpened. The
more fully he came to see the Church, the more fully his
vision justified his having left the Church which he had been
shown and had seen in his youth. He would not even allow
that he had 'evolved'.* He describes the process which led
him to see once again that he was a Catholic, and in fact
that he had never really left the Church, as a process of
approfondissement, a deepening of mind and heart: not a
revolution asserting the contrary of what had gone before,
but a renaissance renewing all that was permanent. The
culmination of that process is only described once in Péguy's
work, with perfect clarity, not, significantly enough, with
reference to Christianity, but with reference to his poetry,

---

* It would be impossible to give the reasons with which Péguy substantiates
his claims in this brief introduction. Those who wish to consider his attitude
will find it examined in greater detail in *Péguy* (Harvill Press), where I have
developed the suggestions put forward here. Péguy's original intention, on his
return to the Church, had been to put all his poetry into the same form as the
Jeanne d'Arc (1898) in order to emphasise the continuity of his thought.

in his *Commentary on 'Eve'*, his last poem. The intellectual aspect of his return to Catholicism is in fact clear, but its inmost secret could only be told indirectly, as reflected in the release of his imagination. That is, moreover, the method of the *Biographia Literaria*, where the story of Coleridge's conversion from Unitarianism to faith in the Trinity proceeds intellectually, so to speak, and directly, up to the point at which his rejection of the theory of the association of ideas led him to formulate his conception of the Imagination as a mirror in which to express the culmination of the *approfondissement* in which he came to believe in the Trinity.

'The poet, described in ideal perfection,' Coleridge writes, 'brings the whole soul of man into activity, with the subordination of its faculties to each other, according to their relative worth and dignity. He diffuses a tone and a spirit of unity that blends and (as it were) fuses, each into each, by that synthetic and magical power, to which I should exclusively appropriate the name of Imagination.'

The culmination of Péguy's process is described in different terms and without reference to the imagination, perhaps because Péguy regarded his conception of poetry as classical, equally opposed to the sterilities of order (classicism) and a disorderly fertility (romanticism). But the fact described is the same: the *fusion* of all the faculties, which brings the whole soul into *activity*, to which Péguy would have added that this represented the essential form of liberty. Writing in the third person Péguy speaks of descending to the depths of reality.

'Just as in the matter of faith Péguy descended to the depths at which liturgy and theology, that is to say the spiritual life and the spiritual proposition, are not yet distin-

guished, so, as a writer, he descended to the depths where
the image and the idea are still joined in a liaison which is
itself carnal and not as yet resolved.'

Indeed the whole of the *Commentary* is a gloss on Cole-
ridge's ideas.

To Péguy the poetic act is the imaginative vision, itself
the product of the 'whole soul of man' with all its faculties
fused, so that as Coleridge says, he *diffuses* that spirit of unity
upon his work, and that unity is its form. *Tout le jaillissement
est dans le germe, tout l'ordre dans l'épi*. All the activity, all
the freedom is in the spiritual seed, all the order in the
fruit. Order is the fruit of freedom, that is Péguy's descrip-
tion of his poetry and of his faith, his Catholicism.

The special character of Péguy's poetry—its simplicity—
is the immediate reflection of his faith: simplicity here being
the unity created by the fusion of understanding of which
Coleridge speaks and not the sham simplicity of naïveté.
This reveals a second consideration, where Péguy is again
at one with Coleridge.

Péguy's faith was not in any sense a private affair: his
faith is the faith of the Church, the personal appropriation
through faith of the mysteries revealed. He has neither
private views nor private interpretations to offer. There is
nothing esoteric or 'mystical' about his *mystique*. It is per-
sonal: which means to say that it turns him away from his
private world, releases him from his private world, and
turns him towards others. Faith to Péguy is communion;
poetry to Péguy is communication. His poetry is the direct
communication of the vision given in faith. This directness
of vision attains such clarity for Péguy that he does not
hesitate to put the greater part of his poetry, the main part
of his poetry, into the Mouth of God—as though to illustrate

Coleridge's definition of imagination as 'a repetition in the finite mind of the infinite act of creation in the infinite I AM'. For faith, in Péguy's poetry, is not 'belief'—which at once suggests propositions—but the capacity to see, a light. The choice of faith as a subject was, as Coleridge desired, the choice of a subject 'remote from private interests' while at the same time the centre of his personal life.

The well known distinction which Coleridge draws between imagination and fancy, in the *Biographia*, and which he applies to Wordsworth, applies even more forcibly, I think, to Péguy (not, to repeat, in praise of Péguy or in disparagement of Wordsworth but simply as indicating the character of Péguy's work).

'Last and pre-eminently,' Coleridge writes, 'I challenge for this poet the gift of Imagination in the highest and strictest sense of the word. In the play of *fancy* Wordsworth, to my feelings, is not always graceful and sometimes recondite.' Péguy is not recondite in his allusions, but he is frequently ungraceful and he is in constant danger of falling, like Wordsworth, into sentimentality; then the imaginative structure is obscured, the unity diffused over the poem hidden. In fact, it would be possible to point to the recurrence of certain images in both Wordsworth and Péguy, in particular, children and childhood, which leads them on to very thin ice. Moreover, Péguy was quite unable and certainly unwilling to correct, cut and improve his work. Unlike Wordsworth who could improve the *Prelude* long after he was incapable of conceiving it, Péguy was lacking in technical mastery and adopted a *quod scripsi scripsi* attitude to his work which is responsible for half the trouble. But where imagination is concerned, in the strict Coleridgian sense, Péguy ventured further than Wordsworth (not necessarily more successfully) and gave full expression to the whole range of his imaginative vision in a single, unbroken epic, *Eve*, which, in conception though by no means in execution, sustains the comparison which he did not hesitate to make with the Divine Comedy.

It is probably the exclusion of the poet's private world, the choice of a subject 'remote from private interests' which makes Péguy's work strange. On the other hand the subject being Christianity, it is natural and easy to identify his poetry with the familiar attempt to return to past forms, and even deliberate archaism. There are, no doubt, certain elements in his poetry which make this view plausible—the use of older forms of words, and to a certain extent the *mise-en-scène*—but in general Péguy's style is wholly his own and his *vers libre*, as well as his four-square quatrain, is his own. With the exception of Victor Hugo there is no obvious derivation, and neither Baudelaire nor Rimbaud, the real rejuvenators of French poetry, touched him at all.

Looked upon as a whole Péguy's poetry sprang out of his prose in the same way that his Catholicism grew out of his deepest thoughts and feeling. He found himself a poet just as he found himself a Catholic, and for the same reasons. There was no break with the past and no 'conversion'. His poetry is not a naïve statement of his faith, a simplification, but an infinitely richer and more complete expression of his mature faith or more precisely of the faith which he rediscovered when he left his despairs behind him and discovered the meaning of hope. For it was then that he discovered in hope the parallel to freedom.

There is also a special sense in which Péguy's poetry is the fulfilment of his prose works. It is the proper expression of his *mystique*. And yet in the ordinary sense Péguy is not a mystical poet because his conception of mysticism is perhaps the distinctive mark of his work as a whole.

Mysticism to Péguy is the contemplation of the mysteries of the faith as the spring of action. Anything which smacks of quietism, of passive oriental mysticism, and really of mysticism as it is usually conceived, was anathema to him.

He does not recollect in tranquillity: The Catholics, he wrote, are unbearable 'dans leur sécurité mystique'. The essence of mysticism was an *angoisse* pushing him to action. This action was the communication of his *mystique* as the source or, as he says, the nourishment of life, so that he could write that *la mystique* is the source of *la politique* and that a *politique*, once it becomes detached from its *mystique*, hardens into an ideology and is no longer free to grow and live. Once a *mystique* turns back upon itself to become attentive to its own phases and moods, it becomes a refined form of individualism. The importance of St. Joan in Péguy's work is that she exemplifies the correct relation between *la mystique* and *la politique*, the relation at the basis of the idea of Christendom, not as a fixed form but as a developing communal life. At first Péguy had hoped that Socialism was to replace the stagnant Catholicism of his day. When the optimism of the Socialist idea proved in the Dreyfus Affair to have been an illusion, and it appeared to him as a *politique* divorced from its original *mystique*, he thought in terms, not of a return or conversion to Catholicism, but of a Catholic renaissance. His poetry is the result.

Péguy's *mystique* is not esoteric but popular and his poetry conforms to his *mystique*. He is not concerned with his religious experience, and except in some of the *Quatrains* and the *Sonnets* there is relatively little reference to his belief, his private life or himself. *Credidi, propter quod locutus sum; ego autem humiliatus sum nimis*. He believed and therefore he had to speak, however humiliating his own position, technically outside the Church and deprived of the sacraments owing to his civil marriage. But in order to speak, in order to express the whole gamut of his thought and feeling, he had to find a new voice and a new language: the language of the imagination.

A Catholic renaissance, if it was to mean anything, must involve the whole man, and this was where Péguy reached a conception of the imagination which is parallel to that of Coleridge and Newman. Moreover, the de-christianisation of France which bulks so large in his work, was not, in his view, the result of an intellectual defeat, or of a lack of arguments, but of the intellectualisation which reduced the faith to a series of propositions. It was not arguments which were wanting but charity, life. The individual in that world was isolated and *déraciné* by an excessive intellectualism, by which he meant what Pascal calls *l'esprit de géométrie*, the geometrical and mathematical thought of his day. This tendency had in fact infected both Catholicism and Socialism so that both were reduced to abstractions, and faith, in Newman's terms, tended to be restricted to a notional belief in propositions arbitrarily divorced from life and freedom and in practice from hope. That is why hope is the great theme of the *Three Mysteries* the source and sign of life and freedom to create. But what Péguy desired was a faith in which the spiritual proposition and the spiritual life (while remaining distinct) should never be separated at the root, and to communicate his thought he had to find a language in which the image and the idea would, in the same way, remain vitally linked together: the language in fact of the

imagination. Systematic thought is usually the systematic
exclusion of the image, which becomes at the most an
illustration, and it was Bergson's attempt to bring movement
into thought, and to think in terms of movement and life,
that won Péguy's lasting admiration.

The central image in Péguy's poetry is the fact that it is
God who speaks, and his imaginative power must be measured
by the fact that it can communicate and hand down the
word of God as something new. The reunion of tradition
and freedom is one of Péguy's great themes. For in a pro-
positional Christianity everything which is new tends to be
regarded as false to tradition, whereas in poetry the old and
stale is dead. In the communication of Christianity tradition
and freedom must be united, and the old must be new in a
real and vital sense in order that a notional faith should be
backed by a real assent. Otherwise the notion, though held
intellectually, ceases to have meaning and becomes the end
term of a logical series. That was the criticism which Péguy
made of the intellectualist Catholicism of his day.

But poetry is no more to be found in a sterile order
(classicism) than in a disorderly fertility (romanticism).
Péguy's order is the fruit of freedom, and it is worth
observing that his poetry is both freer than his prose (from
idiosyncrasies) and more orderly, and he regarded himself
as in the classical tradition (of Corneille, not Racine).
Indeed, Péguy points to the poverty of his poetry (the
adjective, the evocative phrase is almost absent) as the mark
of its classicism and of its Christian note. But while the
arbitrary distinction between classical and romantic which
Péguy adhered to serves little purpose, it remains true that
his conception of order as the fruit of freedom is the essential
romantic contribution to criticism. And from that point of

view Péguy could be said to have rediscovered the romantic movement, though not its specific form, romanticism.

There is another respect in which Péguy can be best understood as carrying forward the central ideas of the romantic movement—a movement, be it noted, which in its truest forms made possible the renewal of the link between Christianity and the culture of that time. The ideal perfection of the poet, Coleridge writes, is to diffuse the tone and spirit of unity upon his work 'by that synthetic and magical power' to which alone he reserves the name of imagination. The term of Péguy's poetic work is the poetic synthesis which takes form in the epic. Whatever the weaknesses of *Eve*, and there are many, it is ultimately in his epic that the characteristic quality of his work appears to the full. This note is present from the first, and the three *Mysteries* (*The Mystery of the Charity of Joan of Arc*, *The Porch of the Mystery of the Second Virtue*, and *The Mystery of the Holy Innocents*) are a single poem having for their theme the mysteries of faith, hope and charity. The *Quatrains* offer a parallel with their treatment of the Supernatural and Cardinal Virtues. But in neither poem does Péguy allow himself the scope and the canvas to give his imagination time to focus the whole Christian scheme into a single whole. This was only attempted in his last work, *Eve*, which in a sense represents a fusion of the two forms previously used, the broad imaginative conception of the *Mysteries* being set in formal rhyming quatrains. *Eve*, Péguy claimed, was the only Christian epic which owed nothing to the past, and if criticism ever takes his work seriously it will have to turn to *Eve*.

The epic quality in Péguy's work is not revealed in the size and scope of his work only, but in a radical simplicity which reflects the fullness of the synthesis. For what is restored in Péguy's poetry—and this is the reason for its popular character and for such popularity as he has won—are the unity and simplicity of the Christian vision. It was that vision which had been erased from men's minds and his poetry erupts the moment he tries to communicate it once again, not as it was seen in the thirteenth century but as it is seen now. This simplicity is both freed from 'private interests' and consequently freed to see, which is faith. For if everything in Péguy were to be traced back to one source it would be to what Rolland called his *passion maladive de la liberté*, the passion which made him understand his own times and in the end be understood by it. Freedom to Péguy is the condition of grace and grace itself the source and fulfilment of freedom, for freedom is at the same time the condition of all creative work.

Péguy's poetry, then, may be said to face away from the individual and the poles of his thought are those of Christianity: the personal and the community, the Church. For this reason his poetry is *sui generis*, with few if any links with modern poetry, and having for its characteristic note the objective tone of the epic. These seem to me to be the basic factors in reading and appreciating his poetic work and the starting-point for criticism. He is at the opposite pole from a writer like Rilke and most moderns: not necessarily a greater poet, but a different kind of poet; one to whom poetry is man's first language.

POEMS

Castles of the Loire

ALONG the curving hills and in noble valleys
Like festal street altars the castles have been sown,
And in the majesty of evening and of dawn
The Loire and her vassals advance through those alleys.

Six score castles furnish a courteous array,
Finer, firmer than any palaces we know,
Their names are Saint-Aignan, Langeais, Chenonceaux,
Valençay and Chambord, Le Lude, Amboise, Azay.

And among those castles, I can tell you of one,
Which stands even higher than the castle of Blois,
Than that lofty terrace where the last of the Valois
Used to gaze at the glory of the setting sun.

The vaulting is lighter, the moulding has more art,
The lacy stone more durable and more austere.
And decency and honour and death graven there,
Have inscribed their history in that orchard's heart.

For on that river's banks remains the memory
Of a child who guided her horse towards the stream,
Her coat of mail was new, her soul was all agleam,
In innocence she rode towards her destiny.

For that young girl ere many days should come and go,
(The same who from Touraine her pilgrimage began)
Controlling with a word recruit and veteran,
Rode downstream towards Meung or upstream to Jargeau.

Presentation of the Beauce to Our Lady of Chartres

Star of the sea, behold an ocean of wheat
 And its billowing swell; a cloth beneath the sky
 And the glancing foam, and our granaries piled high
Here you may overlook an ever-spreading sheet.

Here is your voice, on all this plain's dull length,
 And our absent friends and hearts like an empty town,
 Behold our unclenched fists, unneeded hanging down
And all our lassitude and our reserves of strength.

Star of the morning sky, O Majesty unknown,
 Behold outspread the plain of our poor devotion,
 And behold our heavy sorrow, like an ocean
As we march towards your court and glorious throne.

Beyond the horizon's rim a sob is swelling,
 The scanty roofs like groups of isles appear,
 The ancient belfry drops a warning faint and clear,
The sturdy church is like a low-built dwelling.

Sailing to your cathedral city thus we go,
 A rosary of stacks emerges here and there,
 As circular as towers, opulent and rare,
Like forts on a flagship, ringed against the foe.

An endless reservoir for ages yet to come
 Two thousand years of work have conjured from this soil;
 A thousand years of grace have conjured from this toil
For solitary hearts an everlasting home.

You see us marching along this highway straight,
   The rain in our teeth, bespattered with mud and dust
   Upon this ample fan opened to every gust,
The broad highway has become our narrow gate.

We go straight forward without any false pretext
   Or special outfit, our hands hanging by our sides,
   Unhasting and unresting with slow and steady strides,
From fields which are nearest towards fields which are next.

You see us marching on, we are the infantry,
   One step at a time is the most that we advance,
   But two thousand years of the people and the Kings of France,
With all their hangers-on and with all their panoply,

With their feathered hats and their servitors about,
   Have learned to know their way and what it is to choose,
   How one marches forward, one's feet stuck in one's shoes,
The evening of a battle, to the ultimate redoubt.

We were born for you on the margin of this plain,
   Where the golden River Loire serenely curves,
   And this sandy glorious stream forever serves
To kiss the sacred hem of your immortal train.

We were born for you on this mighty plateau's edge
   In ancient Orleans, serious and reserved,
   And everlastingly this turbid stream has curved
To wash these gentle slopes and flow beneath this ledge.

We were born on the border of your level Beauce
   And longtime we have known, from earliest days,
   The entrance to the farm, the peasants' stubborn gaze,
The spade and trench and village with its close.

THE HOLY INNOCENTS

We were born on the border of your level Beauce
    And longtime we have known, from our earliest regrets,
    Whene'er a sun before a scarlet curtain sets
How much despair it hides and secret loss,

And unavoidably it comes to earth at length,
    Earth hard as justice, level as a table,
    Even as a cross-bar, as law equitable,
Like a pond enclosed and yet open like a plinth.

A man from this fertile glebe, who once lived near,
    Had struck the source of a single inspiration,
    A single effort and single elevation,
And raised to your renown the spire without compare.

Tower of David, here is your Beauceron Tower
    The hardest ear of corn that has ever grown
    Towards your peaceful sky and compassionate throne,
And in your heavenly crown the fairest flower.

From the level ground up to the foot of the cross,
    A countryman of ours has made this wonder spring,
    Higher than any saint, higher than any King,
The irreproachable spire which knows not change nor loss.

This is the sheaf and the corn which can never die
    Which will not fade in the sunbeams of September,
    Which will not freeze in the rigours of December,
This is your witness and your servitor for aye.

This is the stalk and ear which never can decay,
    It will not wither when the summer scorches hot,
    And in a rainy winter it will never rot,
It will not be shaken though all men pass away.

POEMS

This is the stone without a stain, or fault.
  Never was a prayer that carried greater weight,
  And never was an argument that went more straight,
And never taller line soared to a boundless vault.

This, which will not die the day that others perish,
  The pledge and likeness of all our abnegations,
  The plan and figure of all our restorations,
Distaff and wool of the humble fate we cherish.

We are travelling to you from far-off Paris,
  For three days we have left our shop and stock
  And the lean Sorbonne with its miserable flock,
Its scientific research and all such worries.

Others will come to you from faraway Beauvais
  —For three days we have left behind our little store
  And the colossal town with its gigantic roar—
Others will come to you from faraway Cambrai.

We come towards you from Paris, the capital,
  There is the centre of our administration
  And our wasted time and our procrastination
And our liberty, so deceptive and so total.

We are coming to you from the other Notre-Dame
  The one which rises from the heart of the City,
  In her royal raiment and in her majesty,
In her own magnificence and her truthful calm.

Just as here you look down on an ocean of wheat,
  Over there it's an ocean of heads you control,
  And the harvests of joy and the harvests of dole
Are collected each night in the courts round your feet.

25

THE HOLY INNOCENTS

From noble Hurepoix we make our way to you,
   An outpost of the Beauce for our frequentation.
   The fields and the farms have a similar formation
But the curtains of trees more often cut the view,

And the fields are more often sundered there by valleys,
   For the Yvette and Bièvre and their additions,
   For their knowing twists about and their emissions,
And are marked by noble châteaux and by long, straight alleys.

But great or small, it is always France the same,
   The country of vines and rivers ever-flowing,
   The country of moors with broom and heather growing,
The country of fine wheat set in a perfect frame.

From far-off Palaiseau we come to your abode,
   From Orsay, suburban, by Gometz-le-Châtel,
   Sometimes called St. Clair; it is not a castle
But a village beside an upward-curving road.

We came out on the plain after climbing this ledge,
   And to Gometz-la-Ville, on St. Clair looking down;
   It is only a village, no signs of a town,
And it stands where the road cuts the plain, on the edge.

We came down where the hillside of Limours declines,
   We met on our way three or four of the police,
   And they glanced at us, showing some marks of unease,
As we paused at the cross-roads to question the signs.

At night we came to Dourdan and stayed there to sleep,
   A large provincial borough, prosperous and strong;
   There, gazed at like a prince, we proudly strolled along
Beside the ancient castle, whose moats are wide and deep.

A friendly household greeted us fraternally,
  The boy's room was given us, and our bed prepared,
  Twenty years of memories that union shared;
And there our bread was cut for us maternally.

Our youth was present, in all of its solemnity,
  Four centuries of honour without reproach,
  Made of those sheets the cover to an eternal couch,
And over us was said a Benedicite.

We acted the part of the jolly traveller,
  Of a boon companion who knows every turn;
  Who has roamed far and wide and has nothing to learn,
But enjoys the world in the rôle of a wanderer.

Beneath the lamp the table glittered white,
  They showed us the kitchen-garden, and the trellised vines,
  And beyond the orchard stood in goodly lines;
Such was our shake-down and bivouac for the night.

The garden was enclosed in an angle of the Orge,
  A wall stood on the right, in creeper-covered shade;
  Above, the waving boughs an airy archway made;
In front were the blacksmith's shop, the anvil and the forge.

We rose up before dawn to journey anew,
  The weather seemed fair, though day had not yet broken,
  With grateful hearts our farewell words were spoken,
But we breakfasted first on a savoury stew,

Because it's agreed that a pilgrim of right spirit
  Should do his fair share of all eating and drinking
  And not of his duties forever be thinking,
For getting up early is quite enough merit.

THE HOLY INNOCENTS

Daybreak was coming, the darkness had scattered
   When we passed through the village of Saint-Mesme and the others
   And our feet marched forward like two friendly brothers,
Left-right and left-right was the business that mattered.

We crossed the Longroy ford and climbed the hill again,
   Henceforward we have finished with our turpitude
   And the iniquity in each vicissitude;
Before us lies the just and unrelenting plain

Where waits the secret terror of our solitude,
   Here are the oxen yoked, the wagon and the byre,
   And here the level dust and equitable mire,
Distress and disarray in equal magnitude.

Spread out before us now, the high-built terrace lies,
   Where nothing hides the man standing before God's face,
   This plain where no disguise, whether of time or place,
Can save the prey who from the heav'nly hunter flies.

Here is the mighty sheaf, the mighty stock,
   The grain between the mill-stones, our subjugations,
   The scanty gleanings and our renunciations,
And the immense horizon on which we look.

Worthless we contemplate that solid space,
   And our servile fear at such a crucial moment,
   And the lawful terror and the secret torment
When we find ourselves alone before your face.

But behold, you stand before us, heavenly Queen,
   How could we have allowed ourselves to be deceived?
   We walked towards you, yet you were not perceived,
Must we forever be unready for the unforeseen?

POEMS

This country is flatter than the flattest table,
    Scarcely the slightest crease or the least depression.
    It is the deed accomplished, the judge in session,
Decree without appeal, rule inevitable.

It is the enunciation without redress,
    The measure overflowing, the fate well filled,
    The steady, settled life; and it is the herald,
And the royal seal with its august impress.

But you are appearing, O mysterious Queen,
    That point down there among the undulations
    Of harvests and woods, and within the fluctuations
Of the far horizon, is not some evergreen,

Nor the silhouette of some familiar tree;
    It is higher and lower and more distant still,
    It stands as firm as hope on the final hill,
On the final slope your peerless spire we see.

Only the road, O Queen, from us to you;
    This is our business, many roads we have known,
    You have your proper glories, we have our own;
The barrier is breached, in time we shall be through.

We know what each kilometre means on the march,
    And how best to use our muscles to struggle on,
    And how each lap is added to the lap already done;
To-night we shall enter by the bridge and the arch,

The moat which encircles your ramparts will be crossed,
    The cars go roaring by, as we walk in the wind,
    This is the country where the camera is blind,
Here is the bare and steady road, from post to post.

THE HOLY INNOCENTS

We were lucky to leave at such an early hour,
　To-night, a few steps from your doorway we shall rest,
And in this ancient, modest inn a frugal guest,
We shall sleep in the shadow of your splendid tower.

By the open window we shall sit in a chair,
　Utterly exhausted in body and in soul,
　With smarting eyeballs, blinking like an owl,
We shall be so weary that we shall only stare;

We shall stare, with eyebrows arched in admiration,
　At the angle only one man has ever found,
　And that unique ascension, powerful and profound,
We shall be worn out and lost in contemplation.

Here is the axis and line and giant blossom,
　Here is the steep ascent and all serenity,
　Here is exactitude and unanimity,
And a stern sorrow, Queen of the piercèd bosom.

Here is true nudity and all else is raiment,
　Here is true raiment, all else is decoration,
　Here is purity, all else contamination,
Here is poverty, all else is ornament.

Here is the only strength, and all else is weakness.
　Here is the very backbone, all else is imitation,
　Here is nobility, all else is degradation,
Here is the only grandeur, all else is baseness.

Here is the only unforsworn fidelity,
　Here is the only leaping inspiration,
　Here is the only moment worth enumeration,
Here is the only plan of durability.

Here is the record, all else is substitution,
   Here is our love and here is our ability,
   And our special bearing and our tranquillity
And lacy carving and careful execution.

Here is the vow, and all else is a treachery
   Here is the reward of our eradications,
   The wages given for our incarcerations,
Here is the truth and all else is a forgery.

Here is the firmament and all else is feigning,
   And, before the judgement, here is an agreement,
   And before Paradise, here is an achievement,
Here is the leaf of stone with its careful veining.

Fixed in the straw-covered chair we shall sit in quiet,
   And nothing we shall see and nothing we shall hear,
   Of the tumult of voices and steps on the stair,
Nor in the room below, the innocent riot.

Nor the noisy wagons to market rolling in,
   Nor the outburst of oaths and feigned indignation,
   For in contemplation and in meditation
We shall embrace the spire without a sin.

And we shall not feel our knees as rigid as pegs,
   Nor hunger, nor thirst, nor our renunciations,
   Nor our aching sides, nor our deliberations,
Nor our clothes hanging stiffly on our swollen legs.

So many inns surround us, yet we sit alone,
   We shall not go to supper, nor descend the stair
   We shall not even see, we shall not even hear
The city prostrate round your altar throne.

THE HOLY INNOCENTS

And when we shall awake, at dawn to-morrow,
   It will prove a purifying resurrection,
   The arms of your cathedral our protection,
Crippled by our journey, full of joy and sorrow.

We come, to intercede for that poor young lad,
   Who died like a fool at the passing of the year,
   At the very season, and as the time drew near
When your son was born, with straw and hay for his bed.

O Virgin, his defects were not the worst offences,
   He had only one fault in his young carapace,
   But death, who hunts us down and follows every trace,
Discovered the self-made breach in his defences.

He was born quite near us in our Gâtinais,
   His feet were on the road we are now descending,
   And all we lose he was already gaining,
However, it was he you destined for your prey,

O Death, first vanquished in a cave at morning;
   He had placed his steps in ours (the print was clear)
   But the single failure of a single fear
Permitted death to enter by a hidden turning.

Behold him now secure within your governance,
   You are queen and mother, you can undeceive him,
   He was pure in heart and you will now receive him,
In your protection and in your benevolence.

Beneath your gaze, O Queen, the hidden heart lies bare,
   You know the law of life and of mortality,
   And thus you know, by what unseen fatality
Is woven and unwoven the pursuer's snare.

You listen to the choir and you can track
   The winding and unwinding of the orchestra,
   And know what timber-clearing by the forester
Is needed for the huntsman to deploy his pack.

And thus you know in what deep harbour of the bay
   Is prepared and launched a noble embarcation,
   And by what play of talent and calculation
A trusted prop stands steady or rots away.

And thus you know on what a razor edge depends
   A panic, its fury and its mitigation,
   And by what gentle touch and oscillation
One scale goes upwards, so that one descends.

And how much can cost the grimaces of the mocker,
   And how much is needed of strength and exertion
   To make by the stroke of an unique conversion
Of a hapless victim an unhappy victor.

Mother, behold him now, he was of our race,
   And twenty years after, he was our renascence,
   O Queen, restore him in his convalescence,
Where death has passed there is room enough for grace.

For us, we shall go back through a land that has no shade,
   Like a castle barren of recess or crypt,
   Limned more precisely than a perfect manuscript,
And so we shall retrace the journey we have made.

Et nunc et in ora for ourselves we entreat
   Who are greater fools by far than that poor young creature,
   You hold us less surely, we are less pure in nature,
And further away from your heavenly feet.

THE HOLY INNOCENTS

When we have finished acting our final personage,
  When we have laid down our fantastical array,
  When the mask and cloak at last are thrown away,
Then deign to remember our lengthy pilgrimage.

When we shall return to that cold and dark abode
  As it was prescribed for the primitive Adam,
  O Queen of Saint-Chéron, Saint-Arnould and Dourdan,
Deign to remember this solitary road.

When in a narrow grave we shall at last be laid,
  And after absolution and the requiem Mass,
  Deign to remember this long pilgrimage in Beauce,
O Queen of all vows to whom our vows are made.

When the pack is laid down and loosed is the cord
  When we shall have sighed our final trepidation,
  When we shall have croaked our final respiration,
Deign to remember your *miséricorde*.

We ask you for nothing, refuge of the sinner,
  But the lowliest place in your purgatory,
  To lament for long on our tragic history,
And to gaze from afar at your youthful splendour.

A Prayer in Confidence

WE do not ask to fold the linen cloth once more
Nor that it should again upon the shelf be placed,
We do not ask that mem'ry's creases be effaced,
To leave this heavy cloak smooth as it was before.

O Mistress of the way and the reunion,
Mirror of justice and the spirit's honesty,
Alone you understand, O lovely Majesty,
The meaning of this halt and this communion.

O Mistress of the race and its divisions,
Temple of wisdom, heavenly rectitude,
Alone you understand, divine exactitude,
The judge, his hesitations and decisions.

When we came to sit at the parting of two ways
And had to choose remorse or else regret,
When before a double fate our feet were set,
When forced upon the crossing of two vaults to gaze,

Mistress of the secret, alone you understand
That one of these two paths led fatally below,
You know the way our steps expressly chose to go
As a craftsman chooses wood for the work on hand.

And not at all from virtue, where we have no part,
And not at all from duty which has never charmed,
But like the steady builder with his compass armed,
We needs must take our stand at sorrow's very heart,

And be firmly placed at the axis of distress,
And by that sacred need to bear a heavier load,
And to feel more deeply and go the hardest road,
And receive the evil at its greatest stress.

By that old craftsman's skill, that capability,
Which will no longer serve us happiness to gain,
May we at least be able honour to maintain
And keep for it alone our poor fidelity.

Prayer to Our Lady of Chartres
For a Credit to be Carried Forward

WE have governed in our time such mighty empires.
O Ruler of Kings and all their institutions,
We have lain so often in stubble and in byres,
O Ruler of vagabonds and revolutions.

We have lost the desire for offices and powers,
O Ruler of dynasties and of expulsions,
We have lost the desire for violent convulsions,
O Ruler of pediments, palaces and towers.

We have fought so fervently in so many wars,
Before the Lord of Hosts and the God of Armies,
We have gained such high renown and glorious scars,
We have crossed so many unsettled territories.

We have lost the desire for soldiering and strife,
Queen of conciliations and disarmaments,
We have lost the desire for a penitent's life,
Queen of seven Sorrows and seven Sacraments.

We have governed in our time such vast provinces,
O Ruler of prefects and of procurators.
We have served unworthily such noble princes,
Queen of votive paintings with their two donators.

We have lost the desire for administrations
And all the prefectures and cities of the earth,
We have lost the desire for great embarcations,
We yearn no longer for the country of our birth.

THE HOLY INNOCENTS

We have made in our time such heavy commitments,
O Key to the sole imperishable greatness,
And we have exhausted such bitter resentments,
O queen of the swearing and forswearing witness.

We have lost the desire for vain resounding words,
Mistress of wisdom and of silence and of shade.
We have lost the desire for gold and silver hoards
O Key to a treasure and bliss which cannot fade.

We have seen so much, O Lady of poverty,
We have lost the desire for any fresh glances,
We have done so much, O temple of purity,
We have lost the desire for any fresh chances.

Refuge of the sinner, we have sinned so greatly,
We have lost the desire for shifts and obstructions,
O Miracle of truth, we have searched so widely,
We have lost the desire for further instructions.

We have learnt in the schools whatever they could teach,
We remember nothing now but your commandments,
We have failed so often in action and in speech,
We remember nothing now but our atonements.

We are those old soldiers who marched across the earth,
Grumbling, yet forever keeping on without relief,
We are that congregation and that knotted sheaf,
We are that race of deep interior worth.

We shall pray nevermore for corruptible lands,
We shall pray for your graces of joy nevermore;
For your graces of honour alone we implore,
We shall nevermore build our houses on the sands.

An eternal edict is all that we can see,
For now we have forgotten everything we read,
And now we have forgotten all that has been said,
We remember nought but your absolute decree.

We have endured too much and now we shall stand fast,
No longer shall we act except in humility
Beneath the rod of an august authority.
O Mirror of times to come and of times long past.

Yet, suppose one day a bankrupt be allowed
To make dispositions and leave a legacy,
If it is not forbidden, O Rose of mystery,
That sums be carried forward by the unendowed;

If a beggar be allowed to choose his succession,
And bequeath the stubble, the straw and the asylum.
If the King may be allowed to bequeath his kingdom,
If the Crown Prince swear afresh on his accession.

If a man be allowed when hopelessly in debt,
To start a fresh account and be given a credit,
And if such an exchange can work without a limit
We ask for nothing on the way that we are set.

If it is agreed that the lowliest debtor,
Though owing everything can freely ask for gold
And can receive a price for what he never sold,
And with his deficit may pay his creditor;

We, who have known but your graces of war,
Your graces of bereavement and graces of pain,
(And your graces of gladness on this heavy plain)
And your graces that walk in the footsteps of the poor;

THE HOLY INNOCENTS

And the long array of your graces of distress,
And fields so hard to plough and muddy beaten tracks,
And wounded hearts and bowed and weary backs,
We ask for nothing, O vigilant Mistress.

We who have known you, only through adversity,
(But may that too be blessed, O Temple of honour)
Deign to carry forward, most generous donor,
Your graces of happiness and of prosperity.

Your graces of unity and peace pour down
On four young heads, a blessing to remain,
And wreathe their brows, O queen of the perfect grain,
With ears of corn, culled from the harvest's crown.

Eve, The Eternal Housewife

From 'Eve'

Jesus speaks:—

O you who track down in their corners and lairs
Dirt and disorder and every impurity,
Every disharmony, every dishonesty,
O mistress of labours, of vigils and of cares,

You set a match to the lamp that you are holding,
The supper table glows beneath its steady rays,
You take this duster to wipe the staircase moulding,
And you arrange the flowers and you arrange the days.

O woman, you arrange the days and all their labours,
And many alternations and vicissitudes,
And governments with their solicitudes,
And the ancient ploughshare and new endeavours.

O woman, you arrange towers and palaces,
And every recantation and iniquity,
And youthful misery and all antiquity,
And ancient tenderness and new embraces.

Women, I say you would arrange the Deity,
If He should choose one day to come within your home,
You would arrange the insult, the heedless blasphemy,
If in this prison God Himself should come.

Women, I say you would arrange the Deity,
If He should chance to pass before your habitation,
You would arrange the outrage and God's supremacy,
If it should come within your observation.

THE HOLY INNOCENTS

Why did you not arrange the heavenly anger,
Why did you not wash clean the iniquitous heart?
Then was the time for it. Why did you not depart,
While yet there was time, from out the pit of danger.

Women, I say you would arrange the thunderbolt
If God should choose to send it down within your home.
You would arrange His grace and the forgiven fault,
If in this prison God Himself should come.

Why did you not arrange the first malediction,
That time it fell on your solitary hearing.
Why did you not include it with your prescription
For ordered government and gentle forbearing.

Women, you would arrange the rites of baptism,
If John should come once more towards another Jordan.
You would arrange the Host and the Holy Chrism,
If man should return to his primitive garden.

Women, you would arrange upon the kitchen shelf,
With the bread which is earthly, the spiritual bread,
Why did you not arrange down to the root itself,
The tree of intellect (before the time had fled).

Why did you not arrange the tree of immortality,
The time that it sprang forth within the deep ravine,
Why did you not arrange the tree of our morality,
The time that it sprang forth upon the hillside green.

Why did you not arrange the bitter crown of thorn,
When nothing could be seen but a timid budding,
Why did you not arrange the snowy-white hawthorn,
When nothing could be seen but a harmless sapling.

POEMS

Why did you not arrange the heavy crimson briar,
When it was only a rose-coloured promise;
Why did you not arrange the heavy Roman ire,
When it was only a newly dawning menace.

Why did you not arrange the sceptre of derision,
When it was still a young and fragile reed,
Why did you not arrange the crown of illusion
When that crown was still a young and fragile weed.

Why did you not arrange (when the early foliage
Of the fragile sapling showed it was not too late),
The judge with double seals, the tree of twofold fate,
Both the tree of the Cross and the fatal tree of knowledge.

Why did you not arrange in that generation,
When it was still a tree of recent date,
The judge with double seals, the tree of twofold fate,
The tree of the gibbet and the tree of salvation.

Why did you not arrange in that dispensation,
Before another law responded to your needs,
The tree of twofold fate, the arbiter of creeds,
The tree of belief and the tree of salvation.

Why did you not wash, O most diligent laundress,
My bloodstained forehead, ere the blood had drowned it,
Why did you not wash, O most careful ancestress,
My face and royal side, ere the spear could wound it.

Why did you not then, O eternally washing
Wash clean my russet beard and my blood-stained tresses.
Why did you not then, O maternally watching,
Support my stumbling footsteps and my distresses.

43

THE HOLY INNOCENTS

Why did you not then, O palsied ancient woman,
When I was insulted and covered with disgrace,
Why did you not then, O poor and shaking human,
Wipe clean the ignominious spittle from my face.

Why did you not then, O industrious charwoman,
For the final repast, the upper room prepare,
Why did you not then, O busy washerwoman,
Wash clean my tangled beard and comb my russet hair.

Why did you not then, O mother and housekeeper,
Sweep away the house where my final meal was laid,
And sweep away the flowers where the final debt was paid,
And sweep away death from my ultimate supper.

Why did you not also sweep away the lictors,
And the injustice enthroned in the tribunal,
And the venal kiss and the thirteenth apostle,
And the lips of Judas saluting the victors.

Why did you not then, O model of womanhood,
Wipe away the sin before it was enacted,
Why did you not, at least within your neighbourhood,
Welcome the Saviour, before he was predicted.

Why did you not then, O my soul, O my mother,
Wipe away the two tears which sprang from these eyes,
Why did you not then, O many times secular,
Receive the only cry which rose to other skies.

*　　*　　*　　*　　*　　*

O women who arrange with a regretful look
A liberation which has now become in vain,
And know how to read in a sordid little book
Your hour-to-hour accounts, the savings and the gain.

POEMS

You were able to arrange the race of prophets,
And the race of saints and the martyrs' blood and fire,
You were able to arrange all the treasures of Tyre,
And the gold amassed for those fabulous banquets.

And all the blood which has dripped from the lions' teeth,
The martyr's blood and the blood of his torturer,
And you could arrange the infamous sepulchre,
And the storm-tossed ship escaped from the jaws of death.

You arrange the defeat as well as the victory,
It is all the same to you, an equal labour.
You arrange activity as well as stupor,
And you are indifferent to an unjust treaty.

The only thing you know is a hostile fortune,
A spy behind the curtain, a watcher at your gate,
The only thing you know is a chance uncertain
And the crushing load of an overwhelming weight.

And your forehead tightly bound with a heavy veil;
And the stillness of night with its shadowy caves.
And the mighty ruins of the down-crashing waves.
And your children afloat on a raft in the gale.

And all is equal to you and all is narrow.
You fear as much the virtuous as the wicked.
And every happiness comes to you crooked.
But every misfortune comes straight as an arrow.

The woods are never green, the waters never flow,
The skies are never pure to your anxiety.
And everything within the universe you know
May be the instrument of infelicity.

THE HOLY INNOCENTS

And all is equal beneath an equal terror.
And nothing you expect from fearful secret things,
And nothing you expect from peoples or from kings
But the slow unwinding of a mighty torpor.

You were able to arrange humanity's despair
And the tetrarch Herod: after he opposed me.
You were able to arrange the sharp Roman spear,
And Pilate and Judas, after he disclosed me.

You were able to arrange the High Priest's presence,
And the soldier Malchus; after he had acted.
And you can arrange both the form and the essence,
You rivet the irons when a man is subjected.

You were able to arrange the hill called Calvary
Or sometimes Golgotha, but when my climb was done,
You arrange gold, brass, crystal and porphyry,
And the key of the treasure, after it is gone.

You were able to arrange the thorny diadem,
The scourge and the sceptre, but when I had been mocked,
You were able to arrange the iron discipline,
The shame and the fury: but when it was unlocked.

You were able to arrange the heavenly hill,
The hill of Sion, but after it had perished,
You were able to arrange that valley as well
Where flowed the Kedron, but after it had vanished.

You were able to arrange the seat of justice
And the Procurator himself: but after the sentence.
And the public benches and the impious outrage
And the turbulent mob: but after the vengeance.

You are able to arrange all jurisdictions.
You listen to all words of interlocutors.
You listen to all legal maledictions.
You listen to the songs of all persecutors.

You knew how to arrange the wood for sacrifice.
The nails and the hammer, but when it had blasted.
You arrange both the prayer and the Holy Office.
And you arrange time, but after it is wasted.

You arrange every terror and ultimate torment.
And you hear the advance of the heavenly ire.
Then you light up the lamp and you stare at the fire.
You arrange the Monstrance and the final Sacrament.

Eternally saving, eternally toiling,
You arrange salvation, but after it is fled.
O woman of medicines, of nursing and healing,
You wipe away the blood, but after it is shed.

Women, I say, you would arrange the Chrism.
You would arrange the altar and the Sacraments.
You would arrange the Pope and his omnipotence,
And mortal sin and heresy and schism.

Women, I say you would arrange the Deity,
And so you did, upon His Incarnation.
You made Him welcome and bowed in salutation
Before the diadem of His authority,

That diadem of thorns cut from the hillside green.
You bowed to the sceptre of humiliation,
You watched the provisional assassination,
And the three tall gibbets sprung from the deep ravine,

THE HOLY INNOCENTS

And the young reed and its cruel prostitution.
You are able to arrange the silent distress,
And every obloquy and every wickedness.
The hair-shirt and the day of dissolution.

You could arrange the victim's expiation—
O women who wept—but after it was finished,
You were able to arrange the interrogation
And the prisoner, but when he had been punished.

You watch the murdered victim at the festival.
You class the proscript along with the proscription.
You watch the triumph of the lofty tribunal
And the unjust judge, before the interdiction.

You watch the offering and the honorarium.
You class the defence beside the prosecution.
O seated in vain below the praetorium,
You watch the lictor's axe of execution.

You class the battle and you class the victory
And you class the accuser along with the crime.
O seated in vain on the doorstep of history,
You watch the consoling defacements of time.

The Resurrection of the Body
From 'Eve'

O WOMAN, you hear me, when the souls of the dead
Shall come again to seek in the ancient parish,
After so much fighting and with so much anguish,
The poor remains of the bodies they have shed;

And when shall arise from the fields of immolation
So many soldiers fallen for cities of earth,
And when from the citadels the guards come forth,
So many aroused from a dreadful hibernation;

And when shall arise with a terrible awakening
So many watchers on the summit of the fort,
When the chamberlains and ladies of the Court
Shall be loosed from the embrace of immemorial slumbering;

When nothing shall be left but dust and ashes blown,
When the Sleeping Beauty shall awake in the hall,
When the Page and the Queen and Prince Charming shall call
—The great day has arrived; O Sire, you must come down;

When all shall tremble, and in the self-same trance,
Shall say: The hour has struck, it is time to come forth,
And when King Louis and when the King of France
Shall be nothing more than the poorest man on earth;

When the bell shall resound no more for baptism,
The beginning of Mass, and the Holy Sacrament,
For the youthful promise and serious engagement,
And the autumn adorned with the grave chrysanthemum;

D   49

THE HOLY INNOCENTS

When the bell shall sound no more for temporal Vespers
The beginning of Mass and august Benediction,
But when we behold without any restriction
The eternal horror of the temporal lepers;

    *   *   *   *   *   *

When the bell shall resound nevermore from the church
To announce to all that the final day is ending,
Nor the angelus ring again for the day's beginning,
And the funeral march before the wedding march;

But when a brass shall resound with a terrible tone,
With a clash that will make the universe to totter,
When Satan with his writhing and monstrous litter,
Shall flee in terror before the Holiest One;

When nothing will be heard but the hollow rumbling
Of a world in collapse like a temporary frame,
When all the globe will seem a deserted building,
Abandoned to decrepitude and open shame;

When the house where the living and the dead belong
Will have nothing left to show but its vacuity,
When the old debate of the feeble and the strong
Will have nothing left to show but its acuity;

When nothing shall be heard but the vast derangement
Of a world which is shaking and falling in space,
And when shall appear the terrible estrangement
Of a soil always settled and solidly in place;

And when shall arise in deserted fields of tares
So many martyrs thrown in the Roman gutters,
And when shall arise a cry that each man utters,
The long remembrance of all his wandering years;

And when in the Close where the tall cathedral looms,
The people set free from a vast necropolis,
In Paris and Rheims and in each metropolis
Shall carry with them still the horror of their tombs,

And when in the public squares they take their stations
And when they shall crowd beneath a final archway,
And when they traverse again the elm-lined pathway
And when they salute again the noble nations;

When they shall assemble in the square called Martroi*,
When they shall gather on the pavements of the towns,
When they salute again their temporal renowns,
And the kingdom at rest beneath the royal sceptre;

When the man from within the oldest tomb has risen
And moved aside the headstone and forgotten urn,
When the oldest torch shall once more faintly burn,
Relit by the blindest ancient in that prison;

When the man who is raised from the oldest urn
Shall brush aside the flowering bush and briar,
And shall ascend again the decaying stair,
Where after every step the silence shall return;

When that man shall seek again in his earliest home
His former body among his former friends,
In the humble graveyard where every journey ends,
Where the dead of the parish and neighbourhood have come;

When he shall know that his relatives are there,
In the church's shadow modestly entombed
When he shall find again beneath the yellow broom
The two square yards of earth which were his rightful share;

* Place du Martroi—principal square in Orleans.

THE HOLY INNOCENTS

When he shall find again all those of his breeding,
And the sons of his sons and all those of his blood,
And the friends of his youth and all his cousinhood
As they came in bands to rejoice at a wedding;

When he shall find, to his school once more returning,
All the friends of his age and the friends of his rank,
And the desk and the master and the august learning
And the map and the cube and the gramme and the franc;

When everyone shall rise and muster on the deck
To sail away in a final embarcation,
When everyone shall rise to founder in a wreck
Where the final rock shall prove a new foundation;

When each shall find again his dwelling and his race,
To be for ever reunited or bereaved,
When each shall recognise intelligence and grace,
To be for ever confiscated or retrieved;

When the flames of memory shall light up that day,
When every man will resemble a spectator
When the whole of creation before the Creator
Will seem like a shroud that's folded and laid away.

When through the cities the risen dead shall wander
Seeking out their way, uncertain and puzzled,
And hand in hand advancing, their eyes half dazzled,
And hardly knowing each turning and meander

Of the paths their youthful innocence had taken,
And still astonished because the day has come at last,
And still assailed by memories of the past,
And hardly knowing, before the dawn shall waken,

Those paths that they followed in their earliest age,
Still lost in amazement to have returned once more,
And hardly knowing these bodies bare and poor,
And hardly knowing this old familiar cottage,

And these flowery paths their youthful feet had followed,
And the lilacs growing in the ancient bowers,
And pinks and roses, so many mortal flowers,
Before they shall ascend to flowers more hallowed;

*   *   *   *   *   *

When they shall advance in that eternal darkness,
Still quite astonished to be thus in their bodies,
Among ancient scruples and remorseful memories
And to have donned once more their fleshly awkwardness,

To have become uncouth and helpless in their limbs,
And quite embarrassed by their re-emergence,
Like a king who returns and is lost in his rooms
And no longer knows his splendid apartments;

Like a king who returns to his old resplendence
And can no longer find his Lord High Chamberlain,
Nor his grand Majordomo and asks for the plan
Of his own royal palace and seeks the attendants

Who could reanimate that grandiose array,
And the throne room and the room of his anointing,
With the golden sword and pearly sceptre pointing,
And in the council room could sweep the dust away

And show to him his royal bodyguard in place,
The marble forecourt and the central portico,
The shady garden where the silver waters flow,
And restore to him his sovereignty of race;

THE HOLY INNOCENTS

When a man shall advance in the starry darkness
Still quite at a loss in his re-incorporation,
When a man shall advance in the gloomy starkness
Still all confounded by this transformation;

When a man shall advance in a silent night,
Still quite amazed to be re-incorporated,
When he shall fix his gaze upon a final site,
Still quite dumbfounded to be thus translated;

When a man shall advance in the night's abysm
Still stupefied to be reintegrated,
Inscribed again and reincarcerated,
Still stunned by the universal cataclysm;

When your long-lost children, O toiling ancestress,
Shall travel the length of their ancient affections,
And the length of their cares which from all directions
Led back to one point and centre of distress

The long meanders of a heart's hesitations,
When they shall recognise the ancient promises,
When they shall find again the former anguishes,
The dust and ashes of a heart's lacerations;

When they shall traverse the wandering ways
Which led them to sorrow and will lead them again,
When they shall travel the length of countless days
Which always led them back to the self-same throbbing pain;

When they shall recognise the days of their distress,
Finer and deeper than the days of their felicity,
When they shall renew their days of fidelity,
Harder and more loved than the days of joyfulness;

When they see the altar and the primitive steps,
When they see the temple and the primitive stair,
When they see the doorway and the sacred marbles
And the Roman brick and vault and arches there

Of the ancient bridge their vanished gladness followed,
When they shall walk on the bank beside the river,
When they shall renew in days now gone for ever,
The days their clumsy innocence had hallowed;

When they shall advance all the length of the rampart,
When they shall gaze at the chimneys towering high,
Quite awkward and adrift and stricken through the heart,
By recollection of the years gone by;

And when the gleaners shall awake in the field,
Who in mortal sin have fallen into dust,
But also when the highest patronage shall yield
The first-fruits of a sacramental trust;

When in one place the highest personality
Shall be no greater than the latest guest to come,
When those from the richest and stupidest home
Will be no more esteemed than the poorest family;

When your long-lost children, O Queen of tribulation,
Shall thus advance beside the ancient wood,
When for the final time upon the public road
They set forth but walk in isolation;

When they shall advance along the ancient meadows
In a mood of gentleness and meditation,
When they shall sink down among regretful shadows
Into obsolescence and disintegration;

THE HOLY INNOCENTS

When they shall go forward on their ultimate way
Like the youthful Haemon and fair Antigone,
When the latest cornflower and latest jasmine spray
And sweet periwinkle and chaste anemone

Beneath those latest travellers' feet shall spread
The final expanse of the carpets of the earth,
When vainly flowering and vainly spreading forth,
The fumitory and marsh-grown arrowhead

Shall spread for the feet of that mighty regiment
The final expanse of the winding-sheet of earth
When the hemlock and the snake-weed standing forth
So vainly fortified and vainly vigilant

And vainly dangerous and deep-rooted in their place,
Shall spread for the feet of your last posterity,
Vain in adversity, vain in prosperity,
A sheet for the repose of the ultimate race

And the ultimate passage and the ultimate trace,
The footsteps on the flowers and the footsteps on the sand,
When your long-lost children shall advance through the land
And along the terrace; O mortal ancestress,

For the final footprint and final impression,
And when they shall tread down the lavender and thyme
And when they shall advance in the final dawn of time
Towards the final judge and the final session;

When they shall go in bands behind their parish priests,
When they shall contemplate the final tribunal,
When they shall advance all the length of the canal,
As they would go in bands on holidays and feasts;

POEMS

When through the everlasting night they pass
And leave behind the bakery and village oven,
And the windmill and the field they shared in common
As they went in bands at Christmas to midnight Mass;

When they shall have passed before the blacksmith's dwelling,
And the forge and anvil and the secular array,
When they shall jar against a fruit-tree in the way,
Still stupefied and sleepy, and hardly telling

Those paths they followed in their headstrong innocence,
And when they shall tremble in an ultimate death
Can you furnish a light to illumine their path
In that uncertainty and in that impotence;

Mother of the leper and the grand seneschal,
Can you find again in that huddled profusion
Will you know how to light in that weary confusion
To illumine their footsteps some meagre signal,

And when they shall pass beneath the ancient postern,
Can you rediscover for those ragged urchins,
And those young recruits and those hardened veterans
To enlighten their footsteps, some ancient lantern;

Will you have found with your strength diminished
The little that is needed to shepherd that troup,
And to shepherd those mourners and to shepherd that group
In forgotten tracks of roads that have vanished.

For Those who Die in Battle

From ' Eve '

Happy are they who die for a temporal land,
When a just war calls, and they obey and go forth,
Happy are they who die for a handful of earth,
Happy are they who die in so noble a band.

Happy are they who die in their country's defence,
Lying outstretched before God with upturned faces.
Happy are they who die in those last high places,
Such funeral rites have a great magnificence.

Happy are they who die for their cities of earth,
They are the outward forms of the City above.
Happy are they who die for their fire and their hearth,
Their father's house and its humble honour and love.

That house and its pride are the first inauguration
The image and form of a celestial mansion.
Happy are they who die in that consecration
The pledge of honour and its earthly confession.

That pledge of honour begins a new construction,
The first attempt at another, holier troth.
Happy are they who die in that dark destruction
In the fulfilment of a terrestrial oath.

Happy are they who die for they are enfolded
Into the primitive earth and its rule austere,
They have become once again like the potter's ware,
They have become once again like urns new moulded.

POEMS

Happy are they who die, for they are enfolded
Into their primitive form and their truthful figure,
They have become once more the objects of nature
Which the hand of God Himself drew forth and moulded.

Happy are they who die, for they are enfolded
Into the primitive clay, their lodging of old,
They are remade within that destructable mould
Whence by the hand of God they had been unmoulded.

Happy are they who die. To familiar earth
They return, whence the voice of God awoke them.
They sleep, and alleluias shall once more cloak them
Which they had forgotten ere they were brought to birth.

Happy are they who die, for they are included
Once more in their antique home, their ancient mansion,
They have discovered once more their youthful season
From whence God hurried them forth, poor and denuded.

Happy are they who die, for they have retreated
Into that oozy clay out of which God wrought them,
Into that reservation whence God had sought them.
Happy the discrowned kings and the great defeated.

Happy are they who die, for they have retreated
Into that primitive soil whence God evoked them,
And into that resting place whence God convoked them.
Happy the banished kings and the great defeated.

Happy are they who die. Deep in that oozy earth
Where they have returned and from whence divinely made
In a hosanna they newly are wrapt and laid,
Which they had forgotten ere they were brought to birth.

THE HOLY INNOCENTS

Happy are they who die, for they have retreated
Into the primitive earth, that darkest retreat,
Among the coal beds and peat they fed with their sweat.
Happy the sad-eyed kings and the great defeated.

Happy the mighty victors. Peace to the men of war.
May they be enshrouded in ultimate silence.
May God put beside them in the perfect balance
A little of that soil of filth and dusty ore.

May God put beside them in the perfect balance
That which they loved so much, a handful of their land,
A cutting of that vine, something of that pleasaunce,
A corner of that valley, solitary and grand.

Mother, behold your sons, those warrior natures,
You see them lie outstretched among all the nations.
O may the hand of God on His broken creatures
Be light, on hearts of sadness and hesitations.

And see, in the *battues* the game has been taken,
All the eagles brought down and the hares hallooed forth.
Deal gently, O Lord, with Thy vessels of earth,
With those hearts sorely tested, those limbs torn and shaken.

And may He deal gently with poor thwarted creatures
And recall on that day all His pity and hope
And consider their doom and that gag and that rope,
Those tight-knotted wrists and distorted pale features.

Behold, Mother, your sons, who have battled of old.
May God never weigh them as angels are weighed,
But in mercy weigh with them a handful of mould
Wherein once they were formed and again are remade.

60

Behold, Mother, your sons, from so many affrays,
May they never be weighed in a spiritual scale,
But be judged like an outlaw thrust forth from the pale
Who slinks back to his home through dark overgrown ways.

See, Mother, your sons who continually fought.
May they not be judged in their lonely poverty.
May God weigh with them their meagre territory
Which they loved so dearly, and too dearly had bought.

Behold, Mother, your sons who have wandered footsore.
By a petty intrigue may they never be judged,
Like the prodigal son far away they have trudged,
Yet to welcoming arms may they stumble once more.

May they never be judged by their servitors' station,
Nor like clerks to be asked for a final account,
May they never be taxed as a downtrodden nation
Of whom Cæsar demands the integral amount.

But honoured again, as sons who are nobly born,
Freely installed again in their noble mansion.
Surrounded by fields of maize and by fields of corn,
May they be granted again an upright reason.

In their first young season may they lie at rest.
In their first young springtide may they once more reign.
Like shepherds in their snowy fleeces warmly dressed
May they lead forth their flocks to pasture once again.

And may they return to their primitive village
And again be restored to their primitive truth,
And may they repose in their earliest cottage
And at last re-ascend to their primitive youth.

THE HOLY INNOCENTS

For what we have remade is never well remade,
And everything is ruined by postponement,
But what we have unmade is eternally unmade
And yet nothing is recovered by atonement.

What we have avowed is not honestly avowed,
What we have refused is really turned away,
And what we have allowed is not honestly allowed,
But that which we forbid we finally gainsay.

Whatever we infect will always be impure,
But what remains untouched is never safely stayed,
Whatever we aver is never really sure,
But that which we betray is always well betrayed.

Wherever we submit is no real submission.
Wherever we revolt is a true insurrection.
Whatever we admit is no true admission.
Whatever we reject is a real rejection.

For all wears away and yet nothing is mended,
And the river flows on and will never flow back,
Even life, even death, and the Louvre and the shack,
And none have climbed up and yet all have descended.

May they not be weighed in a spiritual scale,
May they not be condemned by Thy divinity,
May they not be measured against infinity,
But may God put beside them the walls and the shale

And the thin line of bushes which marked out their bourn.
May they never be judged by a primitive right.
May they never be judged in a blinding cold light.
May they never be judged in a primitive morn.

POEMS

May they never be judged as are spirits divine,
May they never be weighed with an equal rigour,
Like the ripening harvest and trellised vine
May they never be weighed in their straggling vigour.

May they never be judged as are spirits of air.
But may they be shrouded in shadow and silence.
May they never be hurtled all wretched and bare
Into the bowl of an equitable balance.

May they never be likened to spirits of snow.
May God recollect in that terrible season
Their arterial blood and terrestrial reason
Whose meanderings were unchangeable and slow.

May they never be judged on a servile deceit,
May they never be weighed with a heavenly weight,
But embraced like the prodigal though he come late
When he throws himself down at the fatherly feet.

Mother, here are your sons. They were foolish and cold,
By their servile fatigue may they never be measured.
May they be like the prodigal once again treasured
When he turns and creeps home along paths known of old.

On a servile design may they not be confounded,
In the Enemy's grasp may they never be drawn.
By Thy love like the prodigal once more surrounded
When he knows his own porch and familiar lawn.

May the Lord show them mercy: forgive them, O Lord!
For loving so dearly their corruptible land.
From it they were fashioned. Of this mud and this sand
Was their primitive substance and scanty reward.

THE HOLY INNOCENTS

It was blood of their arteries, blood of their veins,
And the blood of those hearts which will never beat more.
It was blood of desire and the blood of their pains,
And the blood of regret for the ages before.

May the Lord show them mercy. Forgive them, O Lord!
For loving so dearly their corruptible land.
From it they were mustered; of this mud and this sand
Were their feet of frail clay and their scanty reward.

NOTES ON THE POEMS

The *Présentation de la Beauce* refers to a pilgrimage to Chartres made by Péguy, probably when his son Marcel was ill with diphtheria.

Prière de Report, and Prière de Confidence

These two prayers are from *Les Cinq Prières dans la Cathédrale de Chartres*. They refer to another and probably later pilgrimage to Chartres. Péguy went once by himself, once with Alain Fournier, and once with his son Marcel, according to Marcel Péguy, but the chronology is confused. In any case these prayers refer to a moment of decision in his life, when he 'lost his desire for offices and power' and when his life took a new direction.

The *Prière de Confidence* refers to the emotional crisis in his life. 'Péguy,' Madame Favre (M. Maritain's mother) writes, 'wished to assume all alone, all the suffering of which no one near him had the slightest suspicion; his friend married and had a family and he wished to remain alone to face the disturbing mystery of sorrow.' Péguy had told Madame Favre that he could not allow his vocation to be wrecked by a *dérèglement de coeur*.

The Eternal Housewife

Eve, Péguy's epic, is an unbroken series of quatrains, which fall into a succession of 'climates'. The first climate is the climate of Paradise. These verses are from the second, *le climat du rangement*, the climate of habit and memory, in which everything is arranged and tidied, ordered, systematised: the opposite of the climate of creation and fertility, and spontaneity.

The Resurrection of the Body

The Resurrection of the Body follows immediately on the climate of *rangement* and is followed by the better known 'Heureux ceux qui sont morts pour la terre charnelle'.

THE MYSTERY OF THE HOLY INNOCENTS

TRANSLATOR'S NOTE

I have followed Péguy's punctuation and spacing as closely as possible, though I have sometimes added capitals to abstract nouns in order to make the sense clearer to an English reader. Péguy was his own type-setter and therefore the lettering, punctuation, etc., are idiosyncratic.

I cannot explain his use of capitals for Faith and Charity, while hope is generally without one, but, as this difference was clearly intentional, I have left it unaltered.

All the cuts are marked by asterisks. Most of them are a page or less in length, except for forty-five pages on page 128, where the story of Joseph and his brethren is told in dialogue form between Madame Gervaise and Jeanne. The other passages omitted are repetitions, with little variation, of themes already fully developed.

The Mystery of the Holy Innocents

MADAME GERVAISE

I AM, God says, Master of the Three Virtues.

Faith is a loyal wife.
Charity is a fervent mother.
But hope is a very little girl.

I am, God says, the Master of the Virtues.

It is Faith who holds fast through century upon century.

It is Charity who gives herself through centuries of centuries,
But it is my little hope
Who gets up every morning.

I am, God says, the Lord of the Virtues.

It is Faith who resists through century upon century.
It is Charity who yields through century upon century.
But it is my little hope
Who every morning
Says good-day to us.

I am, God says, the Lord of the Virtues.

THE HOLY INNOCENTS

Faith is a soldier, a captain who defends a fortress.
A town belonging to the King,
On the marches of Gascony, on the marches of Lorraine.
Charity is a doctor, a Little Sister of the poor,
Who nurses the sick, who nurses the wounded,
The poor subjects of the King,
On the marches of Gascony, on the marches of Lorraine.
But it is my little hope
Who says good-day to the poor man and the orphan.

I am, God says, the Lord of the Virtues.

Faith is a church, a cathedral rooted in the soil of France.
Charity is a hospital, an alms-house which gathers up all the
    wretchedness of the world.
But without hope it would be nothing but a cemetery.

I am, God says, the Lord of the Virtues.

It is Faith who watches through centuries of centuries.
It is Charity who watches through centuries of centuries.
But it is my little hope
who lies down every evening
and gets up every morning
and really has very good nights.

I am, God says, the Lord of that virtue.

THE MYSTERY OF THE HOLY INNOCENTS

It is my little hope
who goes to sleep every evening,
in her child's bed,
after having said a good prayer,
and who wakes every morning and gets up
and says her prayers with new attention.

I am, God says, Lord of the Three Virtues.

Faith is a great tree, an oak rooted in the heart of France,
And under the wings of that tree, Charity, my daughter Charity
  shelters all the distress of the world.
And my little hope is only that little promise of a bud which
  shows itself at the very beginning of April.

And when one sees the tree, when you look at the oak,
That rough oak bark, thirteen and fourteen times and eighteen
  times a centenarian,
And which will be a centenarian and venerable throughout ages
  upon ages,
That hard, wrinkled bark and those branches which are like a
  jungle of enormous arms,
(A jungle which is an order),
And those roots which plunge down and seize the earth like a
  jungle of enormous legs,
(A jungle which is an order),
When you see so much strength and so much roughness the
  little tender bud looks like nothing at all.
Then it seems like a parasite on the tree, to eat at the tree's
  table.
Like mistletoe, like a fungus.

Then it seems to feed on the tree (and the peasants call them *gluttons*), then it seems to lean on the tree, to issue from the tree, unable to be anything, unable to exist without the tree. And in fact, to-day it comes out of the tree, at the axil of the branches, at the axil of the leaves and it cannot exist at all without the tree. It seems to come from the tree, to steal the nourishment of the tree.

And yet, from it everything comes. Without a bud which had once come forth, the tree would not exist. Without these thousands of buds which come forth only once, at the very beginning of April and perhaps in the last days of March, nothing would last, the tree would not last, would not hold its place as a tree (and that place must be held), without that sap which rises and oozes in the month of May, without those thousands of buds which pierce tenderly at the axil of the hard branches.

Every place must be held. Every life springs from tenderness.

* * * * * *

The most hardened warrior has been a tender infant nourished with milk; and the toughest martyr, the strongest martyr tortured on the iron horse, the martyr with the roughest bark, the most wrinkled skin, the strongest martyr on the rack and in the thumbscrew has been a tender, milky child.

Without that bud which looks like nothing, which seems nothing, the whole thing would be only dead wood.

And dead wood will be thrown in the fire.

* * * * * *

For it is easier, God says, to ruin than to build;
And to bring death than to bring to birth;
And to kill than to create;

And the bud does not resist at all. That is in fact because it is
not made for resistance, it is not commissioned to resist.
It is the trunk and the branch and that governing root which are
made for resistance, which are commissioned to resist.
And it is the rough bark which is made for roughness and which
is commissioned to be rough.
But the tender bud is only made for being born and is only
commissioned to bring to birth.

(And to make things last).

(And to make itself loved).

And I tell you, God says, without that burgeoning at the end of
April, without those thousands, without that unique little
burgeoning of hope, which obviously everybody can break,
without that tender downy bud, which the first comer can
nip off with his nail, all my creation would be nothing but
dead wood.
And dead wood will be thrown in the fire.

And all my creation would be nothing but an immense cemetery.
And my Son said to them: *Leave the dead to bury their dead.*

Alas my Son, alas my Son, alas my Son;
My Son who on the Cross had a skin as dry as bark;
a faded skin, a wrinkled skin, a tanned skin;
a skin which cracked under the nails;
my Son had been a tender milky child;

THE HOLY INNOCENTS

a childhood, a burgeoning, a promise, an engagement;
an attempt; an origin; a beginning of a Redeemer;
a hope of salvation; a hope of redemption.

O day, O eve, O night of the entombment.
Fall of that night I shall nevermore see.
O night, so sweet to the heart because you fulfil,
And you soothe like a balm.
Night on that mountain and in that valley.
O night, I had said so often I should never see you more.
O night, I shall see you throughout my eternity.
That my will be done. O it was then that my will was done.
Night I see you still. Three tall gibbets were raised up. And my
    Son in the middle.
A hill, a valley. They had started from that town which I had
    given to my people. They were raised up.
My Son between those two thieves. A wound in his side. Two
    wounds in his hands. Two wounds in his feet. Wounds on
    his forehead.
Some women who stood upright weeping. And that bowed head
    which dropped on his breast.
And that poor dirty beard, all soiled with dust and blood.
That ruddy forked beard.
And that soiled hair in disorder that I would have kissed again
    and again.
That beautiful ruddy hair, still bloodstained from the crown of
    thorns.
All soiled, all clotted together. All was accomplished.
He had endured too much.
That bowed head which I would have rested on my bosom.
That shoulder which I would have rested on my shoulder.

And that heart no longer throbbed, which had so often throbbed
with love.

Three or four women stood upright weeping. As for men I don't
remember, I think there were none left.

They had found perhaps that it was too much. All was finished.
All was consummated. It was finished.

And the soldiers went home, and on their square shoulders they
bore the might of Rome:

It was then, O night, that you came. O night, ever the same.

Even so you come every evening and have come so many times
since the earliest darkness.

Even so you came down on the smoking altar of Abel, on the
corpse of Abel, on that torn corpse, on the first murder in
the world.

O night, even so you came down on the lacerated corpse, on
the primal, on the greatest murder in the world. It was then,
O night, that you came.

The same that had come down on so many crimes since the
beginning of the world;

And on so many stains and on so much bitterness;

And on that sea of ingratitude, even so you came down on my
mourning;

And on that hill and on that valley of my desolation; it was then,
O night, you came down.

O night, must it be, then must it be that my Paradise

Will be nothing but a great clear night which will fall on the
sins of the world.

Shall it be thus, O night, that you will come.

It was then, O night, that you came; and you alone could finish,
you alone could bring to an end that day of days.

As you brought that day to an end, O night, will you bring the
world to an end?

And will my Paradise be a great shining night?

THE HOLY INNOCENTS

And all that I shall be able to offer
As my gift and as my offertory
To so many martyrs and to so many executioners,
To so many souls and to so many bodies,
To so many pure and to so many impure,
To so many sinners and to so many saints,
To so many faithful and to so many penitents,
And for so much pain and for so much mourning and for so
    many tears and for so many wounds,
And to so many hearts who have throbbed so much with love,
    with hate,
And to so many hearts who have bled so much with love, with
    hate,
Shall it be said that it must be
That I must offer them
And they will ask nothing but that,
That they will want nothing but that,
That they will have no desire for anything but that,
On those stains and on so much bitterness,
And on that immense sea of ingratitude
The slow fall of an eternal night?

O night you had no need to go and ask permission from Pilate.
    That is why I love you and I salute you.
And among all others I glorify you and among all others you
    glorify me
And you are my honour and my glory,
For you obtain sometimes the most difficult thing in the world,
The surrender of man.
The resignation of man into my hands.
I know man well. It is I who made him. He is a strange creature.
For in him operates that liberty which is the mystery of mysteries.

Still one can ask a great deal from him. He is not too bad. You
must not say he is bad.
If you know how to take him you can still ask a great deal from
him.
Make him give a great deal. And God knows if my grace knows
how to take him, if with my grace
I know how to take him. If my grace is insidious, clever as a
thief
And like a man hunting a fox.
I know how to take him. It's my business. And this liberty itself
is my creation.
One can ask from him plenty of heart, plenty of charity, plenty
of sacrifices.
He has plenty of faith and plenty of charity.
But what one can't ask from him, damn it, is a little hope.
A little confidence, what, a little relaxation.
A little delay, a little abandonment.
A little pause. He is always resisting.
Now you, my daughter night, you succeed, sometimes, you
sometimes obtain just that
From rebellious man.
This gentleman's consent to yield a little to me.
Just to relax, his poor tired limbs on a restful bed.
Just to relax, his aching heart on a restful bed.
For his head, above all, to be still. It goes on far too long, that
head of his. And he calls it work when his head goes on like
that.
And his thoughts, no, for what he calls his thoughts.
For his ideas to be still and no longer shake about in his head
like seeds in a pumpkin.
Like a rattle made from an empty pumpkin.
When one sees what they are, the things he calls his ideas.
Poor creature. I do not like, God says, the man who doesn't
sleep.

THE HOLY INNOCENTS

The kind who burns in his bed from anxiety and fever.
I am in favour, God says, of people examining their conscience,
    every evening.
It is a good exercise.
But then, you mustn't torture yourself to the point of losing
    your sleep.
At that hour the day is done and well done; there is no doing it
    over again.
There is no going back on it.
Those sins which trouble you so much, my boy, well, it was
    very simple.
My friend, you ought not to have committed them.
At the time when you could still not commit them.
At present, it is over, go, sleep, to-morrow you will not begin
    them again.
But the man who goes to bed making plans for the morrow,
Is the one I do not like, God says.
The fool, does he even know what to-morrow will be like?
Does he even know what the weather will be?
He would do better to say his prayers. I have never refused
    to-morrow's bread.
The man who is in my hand like the stick in a traveller's hand,
That is the one who pleases me, God says.
The man who rests in my arms like a laughing baby,
And is not worried about anything.
And who sees the world in its mother's eyes and its nurse's
    eyes,
And who only sees it and looks at it there,
That is the one who pleases me, God says.
But the man who calculates, for to-morrow, who inwardly in
    his head
Works like a mercenary,
Works horribly like a slave turning an eternal wheel,
(And between ourselves like a fool),

THE MYSTERY OF THE HOLY INNOCENTS

Well, he doesn't please me at all, God says.

The man who abandons himself, I love. The man who doesn't
abandon himself, I do not love, it is surely very simple.

He who abandons himself does not abandon himself and he is the
only one who does not abandon himself.

He who does not abandon himself, abandons himself and he is
the only one who does abandon himself.

Now you, my daughter night, my daughter of the great cloak,
my daughter of the silver cloak

You are the only one who can sometimes conquer that rebel
and bend his stubborn neck.

It is then, O night, that you come.

And what you did once upon a time,

You do every time.

What you did one day,

You do every day.

As you came down one evening,

So you come down every evening.

What you did for my Son made man,

O great Charity, you do for all men, his brothers.

You shroud them in silence and shadow

And in healthy forgetfulness

Of the mortal anxiety

Of the day.

What you did once for my Son made man,

What you did one evening among all evenings

O night, you do again every evening for the least of men

(It is then, O night, that you come).

So true it is, so real it is that he became one of them

And that he had bound himself to their mortal fate

And that he became one of them, as it were, at random,

And that he made himself one of them

Without any limitation or measure.

For before this perpetual, this imperfect,

79

THE HOLY INNOCENTS

This perpetually imperfect *Imitation of Jesus Christ*
Of which people are always talking,
There had been that very perfect imitation of man by Jesus
  Christ,
That inexorable imitation, by Jesus Christ,
Of the mortal misery and of the condition of man.

I quite understand, God says, that one should examine one's
  conscience
It is an excellent practice. It should not be abused.
It is even recommended. It is quite right.
Everything which is recommended is right.
And besides it is not only recommended. It is prescribed.
Consequently it is quite right.
But at last you are in bed. What do you mean by self-examina-
  tion, examining your conscience.
If it means thinking of all the stupid things you have done during
  the day, if it means reminding yourself of all the stupid things
  you have done during the day,
With a feeling of repentance, though perhaps I should not say
  of contrition,
But anyway with a feeling of penitence which you offer me, all
  right, that's quite right,
I accept your penitence. You are decent people, good fellows.
But if it means sifting through and ruminating at night over all
  the thanklessness of the day,
All the fevers and all the bitterness of the day,
And if it means you want to chew over at night all the stale sins
  of the day,
Your stale fevers and your regrets and your repentances and
  your remorse which is staler still,

THE MYSTERY OF THE HOLY INNOCENTS

And if it means you want to keep an accurate register of your
    sins,
Of all those stupidities and of all those idiocies,
No, let me keep the Book of Judgement myself.
Perhaps you will be the gainer into the bargain.

*   *   *   *   *   *

. . . When the pilgrim, when the guest, when the traveller
Has trailed for hours through the muddy highways,
Before crossing the threshold of the church he carefully wipes
    his feet,
Before going in,
Because he is very tidy.
And the mud from the roads must not soil the flag-stones in the
    church.
But once it is done, once he has wiped his feet before entering,
Once he has gone in he no longer thinks of his feet,
He is not always looking to see if his feet are properly wiped.
He has no heart, he has no eyes, he has no voice any more
Except for the altar where the Body of Jesus
And the memory and the expectation of the Body of Jesus
Shine eternally.
Only the mud from the roads must not cross the threshold of
    the temple,
Only he must have wiped his feet on the threshold of the
    temple,
Very carefully, very cleanly and don't let's mention it again.
One does not go on talking about the mud. It is not decent.
To carry so much as the memory and anxiety about mud into
    the temple
And the preoccupation and thought of mud
Is in fact to carry mud into the temple,
Now mud must not cross the threshold of the door.

F   81

THE HOLY INNOCENTS

When the guest arrives at his host's let him simply wipe his
   feet before entering,
So that he enters clean and with clean feet and then
He should not always be thinking of his feet and the mud on
   his feet.
Well, you are my guests, God says, and I am worth quite as
   much as the Lord who was the Lord of Hosts.
You are my guests and my children who come into my temple.
You are my guests and my children who come into my night.
On the threshold of my temple, on the threshold of my night,
   wipe your feet and don't let's mention it again.

        *   *   *   *   *   *

Wash and tidy yourself at bedtime. That's what self-examination
   means. One doesn't go on washing all the time.
Be like the pilgrim who takes holy water as he goes into the
   church
And who makes the sign of the Cross. Then he goes into the
   church.
And he does not go on taking holy water all the time,
And the church is not furnished exclusively with holy water
   stoups.
There is that which is before the threshold. There is that which
   is on the threshold,
And there is that which is in the house.
You must go in once and not go in and out all the time.
Be like the pilgrim who sees nothing but the sanctuary,
And who hears nothing else.
And who sees nothing but the altar where my Son has been
   sacrificed so many times.
Imitate the pilgrim who sees nothing but the radiance
Of the glory of my Son.
Enter my night as into my house. For there I have reserved

THE MYSTERY OF THE HOLY INNOCENTS

The right to be master.
And if you are absolutely determined to offer me something
At night when going to bed
Let it be first a thanksgiving
For all the services I do you
For the innumerable benefits which I daily heap on you
Which I have heaped on you this very day.
Thank me first of all, that is the most urgent
And that is also the fairest:
Thereafter let your self-examination
Be a cleansing once for all
And not a dawdling over spots and stains.
Yesterday's journey is done, my boy, think about to-morrow's,
And of your salvation which is at the end of to-morrow's
    journey,
It is too late for yesterday. But it is not too late for to-morrow,
And for your salvation which is at the end of to-morrow's
    journey.

*   *   *   *   *   *

The hour which is striking has struck. The day which is passing
    has passed. Only to-morrow remains and the days after
    to-morrow,
And they will not remain for long.
Then do not in your self-examinations and your penitences
Become rigid and bend over backwards,
O stiff-necked people,
Let them be exercises in flexibility and let your self-examinations
    and your penitences and even your bitterest contritions
Be penitences of relaxation, unfortunate children, and contri-
    tions of resignation
And of remittance into my hands and of surrender,
(Of surrender of yourselves).

83

THE HOLY INNOCENTS

But I know you, you are always the same.
You want to make great sacrifices for me, provided that you can
  choose them.
You would rather make great sacrifices for me, provided that
  they are not those I ask of you
Than to make small ones for me which I do ask of you.
You are like that. I know you well.
You will do anything for me except that little abdication
Which means everything to me.
Then be, in short, like a man
Who is in a boat on the river
And who does not row all the time
And who sometimes lets the current float him along.

In the same way you and your boat
Let yourself go sometimes on the current of Time
And bravely let it float you
Under the arch of the bridge of night.

*   *   *   *   *   *

But when I say to you: Think rather of the morrow I do not
  mean: Calculate about the morrow.
Think of it as a day which will come; and that is all that you
  know about it.
Do not be like the wretch who tosses and burns in his bed
In order to grasp the morrow's day.
Do not put your hand
On the fruit which is not ripe.
Know only that the morrow
Which is always being discussed
Is the day which is to come,
And that it will be in my governance
Like the others.

That is all you need. For everything else, wait.
As for me, God, I have to wait. You make me wait long enough.
You make me wait long enough for repentance after a fault
And contrition after a sin,
And since the beginning of Time I await
Judgement until the Day of Judgement.
I do not like, God says, the man who speculates about to-morrow.
I do not like the man who knows better than I, myself, what I am going to do.
I do not like the man who knows what I shall do to-morrow,
I do not like the man who tries to be clever. The strong man is not my strong point.
Thinking of the morrow, what vanity. Keep for the morrow the tears of the morrow,
(There will always be quite enough),
And those sobs which rise in you and which strangle you.
Thinking of the morrow, do you even know how I shall make the morrow,
What morrow I shall make for you.
Do you know if I, myself, have settled it yet.
I do not like, God says, the man who mistrusts me.
Do you believe that I am going to amuse myself by playing tricks on you like a barbarous despot?
Do you believe that I pass my life setting snares for you and rejoicing to see you fall into them?
I am an honest man, God says, and I always act straightforwardly.
I am honour itself and uprightness and honesty.
I am a good Frenchman, God says, upright as a Frenchman,
Loyal as a Frenchman.
I am the King of France, upright as the King of France.
What the least of the poor would not have feared from Saint Louis, are you going to fear from me?
In short, I am perhaps as good as Saint Louis!

Do you believe I am going to amuse myself with making feints
at you like a duellist?

All the cunning which I have is the cunning of my Grace, and
the feints and the ruses of my Grace, which so often plays
with the sinner for his salvation, to hinder him from sinning;

Which seduces the sinner; in order to save him. But do you
believe. Do you believe that I, God, am going to amuse
myself with inflicting torments on them, which no decent
man would inflict. I am a good Christian, God says. Do you
believe that I am going to amuse myself by surprising them
like a murderer in the night?

*   *   *   *   *   *

I am their father, God says. *Our Father which art in Heaven.* My
Son told them often enough that I am their father.

I am their judge. My Son said it to them. I am also their
father.

I am above all their father.

In short I am their father. Whoever is a father is above all a
father. *Our Father which art in Heaven.* He who has once been
a father can never cease to be a father.

They are my Son's brothers; they are my children; I am their
father.

Our Father which art in Heaven, my Son taught them that prayer.
Sic ergo vos orabitis. Therefore you shall pray thus.

Our Father which art in Heaven, that day he knew very well what
he was doing, my Son who loved them so much.

Who lived among them, who was like one of them.

Who went about like them, who spoke like them, who lived
like them.

Who suffered.

Who suffered like them, who died like them.

And who loves them so much, having known them.

Who has brought back to Heaven, a kind of flavour of man, a
kind of flavour of earth.

My Son who loved them so much, who loves them eternally in
Heaven.

He knew very well what he was doing on that day, my Son who
loves them so much.

When he put that barrier between them and me, *Our Father
which art in Heaven,* those three or four words.

That barrier which my anger and perhaps my justice will never
pass.

Happy is he who sleeps under the protection of the vanguard of
those three or four words.

Those words which go before every prayer as the hands of a
supplicant before his face.

As the two hands of a supplicant advance joined together before
his face and the tears on his face.

Those three or four words which conquer me, me the un-
conquerable,

And which they send in front of their misery like two invincible
hands joined together.

Those three or four words which advance like a strong prow in
front of a weak ship,

And which cleave the wave of my anger.

And when the prow has passed, the ship passes and all the fleet
behind it.

Nowadays, God says, that is how I see them;

And during my eternity, eternally, God says,

By the contrivance of my Son, it is thus that I must eternally
see them.

(And that I must judge them. How would you have me judge
them, at present

After that)?

Our Father which art in Heaven. My Son knew just how to set
about it,

THE HOLY INNOCENTS

To bind the arms of my justice and to loose the arms of my
mercy.
(I do not speak of my anger which has never been anything but
my justice,
And sometimes my charity).
And nowadays I must judge them like a father,
In so far as a father can judge. *A man had two sons.*
In so much as he is capable of judging. *A man had two sons.*
Everyone knows how a father judges. There is a well-known
example.
It is well known how the father judged the son who had gone
away and returned.
Moreover it was the father who wept the most.
That is what my Son told them. My Son yielded up to them the
secret of Judgement itself.
And nowadays this is how they appear to me; this is how I see
them;
This is how I am forced to see them.
In the same way that the wake of a great ship goes on widening
till it disappears and is lost,
But begins with a point which is the point of the ship itself,
So the immense wake of sinners widens till it disappears and is
lost.
But begins with a point and it is the point which comes towards
me, which is turned towards me.
It begins with a point which is the point of the ship itself.
And the ship is my own Son, loaded with all the sins of the world.
And the point of the ship is the point of my Son's hands joined
in supplication.
And before the glance of my anger and before the glance of my
justice
They have all concealed themselves behind him.
And all that immense procession of prayers, all that immense
wake widens until it disappears and is lost.

But it begins with a point and it is the point which is turned towards me,

Which advances towards me.

And that point is the three or four words; *Our Father which art in Heaven*; my Son truly knew what he was doing.

And every prayer rises towards me concealed behind those three or four words.

And there is a point to the point. It is moreover that prayer itself not only textually,

But in its very invention. That first occasion when it was really uttered in Time.

That first occasion when my Son uttered it.

Not moreover only textually as it has become a text,

But in its very invention and in its source and its breaking forth.

When it was itself a birth of prayer, an incarnation and a birth of prayer. A hope.

A birth of hope.

A branch and a germ and a bud and a leaf and a flower and a fruit of speech.

A seed, a birth of prayer.

A word among all words.

That first time it came fort!. in the flesh, in Time, from the human lips of my Son.

And in the point of the point, in that point itself there was a point.

*   *   *   *   *   *

. . . *Our Father which art in Heaven.*

And behind that point advances the point itself, that is to say the prayer in its entirety,

As it was uttered on that first occasion

And behind it widens and disappears

The wake of innumerable prayers

THE HOLY INNOCENTS

As they are uttered textually on innumerable days
By innumerable men,
(By simple men, his brothers),
Morning prayers, evening prayers;
(Prayers uttered at all other times);
So many other times on innumerable days;
Mid-day prayers and prayers throughout the day;
Prayers of monks for all the hours of the day,
And for the hours of the night;
Prayers of laymen and prayers of clerks,
As they were uttered innumerable times
During innumerable days.
(He spoke like them, he spoke with them, he spoke as one of
them),
All that immense fleet of prayers loaded with the sins of the
world.
All that immense fleet of prayers and penitence attack me
Having the prow that you know of,
Advance towards me, having the prow that you know of.
It is a fleet of cargoes, *classis oneraria.*
And it is a fleet of the line
A battle fleet,
Like a beautiful classical fleet, like a fleet of triremes
Advancing to attack the King.
As for me, what do you expect me to do; I am attacked.
And in that fleet, in that innumerable fleet
Each *Pater* is like a high-decked ship
Which has its own prow, *Our Father which art in Heaven,*
Turned towards me, and which advances behind its own prow,
Our Father which art in Heaven, there is nothing clever about that,
Clearly when a man has said that, he can hide himself behind it.
When he has uttered those three or four words.
And behind the grand high-decked ships the *Ave Marias*
Advance like innocent galleons, like virginal triremes.

Like lowly ships which do not offend the humility of the sea.

Which do not offend against order, which follow, humble and
faithful and submissive to the surface of the water.

Our Father which art in Heaven. Evidently when a man has begun
like that,

When he has said those three or four words to me

When he has begun by making those three or four words go
before him:

He can go on, afterwards he can say anything he likes.

You understand, I am disarmed.

And my Son knew it very well,

Who loved men so much.

Who had acquired a taste for them, and for the earth and for
everything to do with it.

And in that innumerable fleet I clearly distinguish three great
innumerable fleets.

(I am God, I see clearly).

And this is what I see in that immense wake which begins with
a point and which by degrees, little by little, is lost on the
horizon of my vision.

They are all one behind the other even those who sheer off from
the wake

Towards my left hand, and towards my right hand.

In front sails the innumerable fleet of the *Paters*

Cleaving and braving the wave of my anger;

Powerfully driven forward by their three ranks of oars.

(That is how I am attacked. I ask you. Is it just?)

(No, it is not at all just, for all this is under the rule of my
Mercy)

And all these sinners and all these saints together go behind my Son

And behind the supplicating hands of my Son,

And they themselves have their hands joined in supplication as if
they were my Son.

In fact my sons, in fact each one a son like my Son.

THE HOLY INNOCENTS

In front sails the heavy fleet of the *Paters* and it is an innumerable
    fleet,
It is in this formation they attack me. I think you understand me.
*The Kingdom of Heaven suffers violence and the violent take it by
    force.* They know it well. My Son has told them everything.
Regnum cœli, the kingdom of heaven. Or *regnum cœlorum*, the
    kingdom of the heavens.
Regnum cœli vim patitur. Et violenti rapient illud.

      *   *   *   *   *   *

And that fleet is more innumerable than the fleet of the Achaeans,
And retreating I recognise the three superimposed decks, the
    three invincible, the three insubmersible decks,
Stronger than the ocean of my anger.
And I recognise the three ranks of oars,
And there are Jewish oars and Greek oars,
And there are Roman oars and there are French oars,
And the first rank of oars is:

(If there is naught but justice who will be saved,
But if there is mercy who will be lost,
If there is mercy, who can boast of being lost.

It is impossible for a man to save himself; but nothing is im-
    possible with God.

From the heights of my promontory,
From the promontory of my justice,
And from the seat of my anger,
And from the chair of my jurisprudence,
In cathedra jurisprudentiae,

THE MYSTERY OF THE HOLY INNOCENTS

From the throne of my eternal greatness
I see rising towards me, from the depths of the horizon I see
  coming
The fleet which assails me,
The fleet deployed in a triangle,
Presenting the point that you know of.

As cranes fly in a triangle upwards,
And in this way go where they will,
Cleaving the air and driving back the power of the wind itself,
So this great triangular fleet
Steals and steers and sails
And so to speak soars
To cross the ocean of my anger.
And the strongest is in front making the point of the triangle.
And they have put themselves behind him one after the other
And one after the other they all disappear from the vision of
  my anger.
They are huddled together in fear; and who would blame them?
Like frightened sparrows they are huddled behind the strongest.
And they present that point to me.
And thus they cleave the wind of my anger and even drive back
  the power of the tempests of my justice.
And the breath of my anger has no longer any effect on that
  triangular formation
In winged flight,
For they present me with an angle and I can only take them
  from that angle.
What are here the Greek fleets and the Persian fleets;
And the Punic fleets and the Roman fleets;
And the English fleets and the French fleets
Forever tossed by the ground-swell of the sea.
Hither sails a fleet which the ground-swell of my anger will
  never toss.

THE HOLY INNOCENTS

And I discover concealed one behind the other an innumerable fleet
And the last are hidden in a mist on the horizon of my vision.
And in that innumerable fleet I discover three fleets equally
 innumerable.
And the first is in front to attack me more fiercely. It is the
 fleet with high decks,
The ships with powerful keels,
Armoured like hoplites,
That is to say like soldiers heavily armed,
And they move invincibly borne on their three ranks of oars).

And the first rank of oars is:
Hallowed by thy Name,
Thine.

And the second rank of oars is:
Thy Kingdom come,
Thine.

And the third rank of oars is the words among all unsurpassable:
Thy will be done on earth as in Heaven,
Thine.

Sanctificetur nomen
Tuum.

Adveniat regnum
Tuum.

Fiat voluntas
Tua
Sicut in caelo et in terra.

And such is the fleet of the *Paters*, solid and more innumerable
 than the stars of the sky. And behind I see the second fleet,

and it is an innumerable fleet, for it is the fleet with white
sails, the innumerable fleet of the *Ave Marias.*
And it is a fleet of biremes. And the first rank of oars is:
Ave Maria, gratia plena:

And the second rank of oars is:
Sancta Maria, Mater Dei.

And all those *Ave Marias,* and all those prayers to the Virgin and
the noble *Salve Regina* are white caravels, humbly lying under
their sails on the surface of the water; like white doves you
could take in your hand,
But those gentle doves under their wings,
Those friendly white doves, those doves in your hand,
Those humble doves lying on the flat of your hand,
Those doves accustomed to the hand,
Those caravels adorned with sails
Of all ships they are the most direct,
That is to say those which reach port the straightest way.

Such is the second fleet, which is of the prayers to the Virgin.
And the third fleet is of the other innumerable prayers.
All. Those which are said at Mass and at Vespers. And at
Benediction.
And the prayers of the monks who mark all the hours of the day.
And the hours of the night.
And the *Benedicite* which is said before dinner
In front of a good steaming bowl of soup.
All, in short, all. And there are no more.

But I see a fourth fleet. I see the invisible fleet. And it is of all the
prayers which are not even said, the words which are not uttered.

THE HOLY INNOCENTS

But I hear them. Those obscure impulses of the heart, the
  obscure good impulses, the secret good movements,
Which unconsciously spring up and come forth and unconsciously
  rise towards me.
Whoever is the source of them does not even perceive them.
  He knows nothing about them and is truly only the source,
But as for me I gather them up, God says, and I count them and
  I weigh them.
Because I am the hidden Judge.

Such are, God says, those three innumerable fleets. And the
  fourth.
Those three visible fleets and the fourth invisible.
Those secret prayers, flowing from the heart; those secret
  prayers of the heart. Those secret impulses.
And assailed so shamelessly, assailed with prayers and tears,
Directly assailed, assailed full in the face
After all this I am expected to condemn them. How easy.
I am expected to judge them. Everyone knows how all such
  judgements end and all such condemnations.
A man had two sons. It always ends in embraces.
(And it is the father moreover who weeps the most).
And in that tenderness which is, which I would put above even
  the Virtues.
Because with her sister, Purity, she proceeds directly from the
  Virgin.

Other galleons, God says, at other times
Other galleons have sailed towards island sanctuaries
And towards temples which were on promontories.

THE MYSTERY OF THE HOLY INNOCENTS

But this time here is a fleet
Assailing the Holy of Holies.

*　　　*　　　*　　　*　　　*　　　*

I have often played with man, God says. But what a game, it is
a game which makes me tremble yet.
I have often played with man but, by God, it was in order to
save him, and I have trembled enough because I might not be
able to save him;
Because I might not succeed in saving him. I mean to say I have
trembled enough for fear of not being able to save him,
Asking myself if I should succeed in saving him.

I have often played with man and I know that my Grace is
insidious, and how much and how often it turns and plays.
It is more cunning than a woman.
But it plays with man and turns him and turns the event and it
is in order to save man and to hinder him from sinning.

I often play against man, God says, but it is he who wants to
lose, the idiot, and it is I who want him to win.
And I succeed sometimes
In making him win.

To speak plainly, we play heads you lose, tails I win.
At least he does, for if I should lose, I lose.
But if he loses, then and then only, he wins.
Singular game, I am his partner and his adversary.

THE HOLY INNOCENTS

And he wants to win against me, that is, to lose.
And I his adversary, I want to make him win.

And the kingdom of *Our Father* is the kingdom of hope itself;
   give us this day our daily bread.

(And the kingdom of the *Hail Mary* is a more secret kingdom).

   *   *   *   *   *   *

Whoever says the prayer, *Our Father which art in Heaven,* places
   between himself and me
An insurmountable barrier to my anger,
And can abandon himself to a night of sleep.
(O night I created you the first). *Thy will be done.*
Besides what I have not done to the outcast races,
Would you expect me to do to my French parishes,
An event has happened in the interval, an event has intervened,
   an event has made a barrier.
Which is the coming of my Son.
And I, where should I be without my old French parishes,
What would become of me. It is there that my name rises
   eternally.
Since when does the general decimate his best troops.
Do you think I am going to surprise my own camp in its sleep.
They are my own men.   Am I going to set about
Decimating my own men.
I should fight a fine battle, afterwards.
Oh, I know very well they are not perfect.
They are as they are. They are my best troops.
You must love these creatures as they are.
When you love someone you love him as he is.
It is only I who am perfect.

THE MYSTERY OF THE HOLY INNOCENTS

That is even, perhaps,
Why I know what perfection is.
And why I ask less than perfection of these poor people.
I know, myself, how difficult it is,
And how many times when they struggle so hard among temptations.
I long, I am tempted to put a hand under their belly
To support them with my broad hand
Like a father teaching his son to swim
In the current of the river
And who is divided between two feelings.
For on the one side if he supports him for ever and if he supports him too much
The boy will rely on him and will never learn to swim,
But on the other if he does not support him just at the right moment
The boy will swallow a nasty mouthful.

*　*　*　*　*　*　*　*

Such is the difficulty, it is great.
And such the very duplicity, the double face of the problem.
On the one hand they must achieve salvation themselves. That is the rule
And it is strict. Otherwise it would not be interesting. They would not be men.
Well, I want them to be virile, to be men and to win
Their spurs of knighthood themselves.
On the other hand they must not be allowed to swallow a nasty mouthful
Having dived into the thanklessness of sin.
This is the mystery of the liberty of man, God says,
And of my management of him and of his liberty.
If I support him too much, he is not free.

99

THE HOLY INNOCENTS

And if I do not support him enough, he will fall.
If I support him too much, I endanger his liberty
If I do not support him enough, I endanger his salvation:
Two goods, in a sense, almost equally precious.
For this salvation has an infinite price.
But what would salvation be if it were not free.
How could it be described.
We want him to gain this salvation by himself.
By himself, by man. Procured by himself.
That it should come, in a sense, from himself. Such is the
 secret,
Such is the mystery of the liberty of man:
Such is the price we put on the liberty of man.
Because I, myself, am free, God says, and because I have created
 man in my image and in my likeness.
Such is the mystery, such is the secret, such is the price
Of all liberty.
This liberty of the creature is the most beautiful reflection that
 exists in the world
Of the Liberty of the Creator. That is why we attach to it,
That we put on it a proper price.
A salvation which was not free, which was not, which did not
 come from a free man would mean nothing to us. What
 would it be.
What would it mean.
What interest could be found in such a salvation.
A beatitude of slaves, a salvation for slaves, a servile beatitude,
 how do you expect that to interest me. Does one love to be
 loved by slaves.
If it is only a question of proving my power, my power has no
 need of those slaves, my power is well enough known, people
 know quite well that I am the Almighty.
My power blazes forth clearly enough in every substance and in
 every event.

My power blazes forth clearly enough in the sands of the sea and
in the stars of the sky.

It is not contested, it is known, it blazes forth clearly enough
in the inanimate world.

It blazes forth clearly enough in the ordering,

Even in the occurrence of man.

But in my animate creation, God says, I have willed better, I
have willed more.

Infinitely better. Infinitely more. For I have willed this liberty.

I have *created* this very liberty. At a few steps from my throne.

Having once known what it is to be freely loved, one no longer
has any taste for subservience.

Having once known what it is to be loved by free men the
prostrations of slaves no longer mean anything to you.

Having once seen Saint Louis on his knees, one no longer desires
to see

Oriental slaves prone on the earth

All stretched out flat on their bellies on the earth. To be freely
loved,

Nothing can weigh as much, nothing can cost as much.

It is certainly my greatest invention.

When one has tasted the joy

Of being freely loved

What remains is nothing but subservience.

That is why, God says, we love these Frenchmen so much,

And that we love them among all, uniquely,

And that they will always be my eldest sons.

They have liberty in the blood. All that they do, they do freely.

They are less slavish and more free in sin itself

Than others in their devotions. Through them we have enjoyed.

Through them we have invented. Through them we have
created

The love of free men for us. When Saint Louis loves me, God
says,

THE HOLY INNOCENTS

I know that he loves me.

At least I know that he indeed loves me, because he is a French
   baron. Through them we have known what it is

To be loved by free men. All the submissions, all the lamentations
   in the world

Are not worth one beautiful prayer from those free men kneeling
   very upright. All the submissions in the world

Are not worth the springing forth

The beautiful straight thrust of a single invocation

Of a free love. When Saint Louis loves me, God says, I am safe,

I know what you are talking about. He is a free man, he is a
   free baron of the Isle of France. When Saint Louis loves me

I know, I understand what it is to be loved.

(And that is everything). Doubtless he fears God,

But it is a noble fear, all filled, all swelled,

All replete with love, like a fruit swollen with juice,

In no way a cowardly, a base fear, an indecent fear

Gripping the belly. But a great, but a high, but a noble fear,

The fear of displeasing me because he loves me, and of disobey-
   ing me because he loves me,

And because he loves me, the fear

Of not being found pleasing

And loving and loved in my sight. No infiltration in that noble
   fear

Of an evil fear and a pernicious and vile cowardice.

And when he loves me it is true. And when he says he loves me
   it is true. And when he says that he would rather

Have leprosy than fall into mortal sin (he loves me so much), it
   is true.

With him I know it is true.

It is not only true because he says it. It is true because he is
   true. He does not only say it to sound well.

He does not say it because he has seen it in books nor because
   he has been told to say it. He says it because it is so.

THE MYSTERY OF THE HOLY INNOCENTS

He loves me to such a pitch. He loves me thus. Freely. The proof
I have from the same race
Is that the Lord of Joinville (whom I love dearly all the same)
who is another French baron,
Who would rather have committed thirty mortal sins than have
leprosy,
(Thirty, the wretched man, as though he did not know what he
was saying)
Does not hesitate either to say what he thinks
That is, to say the contrary
Even in the presence of so great a King
And of so great a Saint
Who nevertheless he knew for such,
That is, to contradict so great a King and so great a Saint. The
freedom of speech
Of the one who will not risk the horror
Of having leprosy rather than fall into mortal sin
Guarantees me the freedom of speech of the other who would
rather have leprosy
Than fall into mortal sin.
If one says what he thinks, the other says what he thinks.
One confirms the other.
They are not afraid to contradict even the King, even the
Saint.
But likewise when they speak, one knows they are speaking as
they are.
And what they think they say. And what they say they think.
It is all one.
What would one not do to be loved by such men.
Servitude is an air which you breathe in a prison
And in a sick-room. But liberty
Is that fresh air which you breathe in a fair valley
And even better on a hill-side and even more surely on a wide,
open plateau.

THE HOLY INNOCENTS

And there is a certain tang in the pure and open air
Which makes strong men, a certain tang of health,
Of full, virile health which makes all other air seem
Shut-up, sick, confined.
He alone who lives in the open air
Has the tanned skin and the deep glance and the blood of his
  race.
So he alone who lives in open liberty
Has the tanned skin and the deep soul and the blood of my
  Grace.
What would one not do to be loved by such men!
As they are frank with each other so are they frank with me.
As they tell each other the truth so they tell me the truth,
And as the baron is not afraid to contradict even the king and
  the saint,
(Whom he loves so much, whom he values at his worth, for
  whom he would die),
So, I admit it, they are sometimes not afraid to contradict me.
Me the king, me the saint. But when they love me, they love me.
They value me at my worth. They would die for me.
I have a guarantee even in their rough liberty.
Their liberty of speech their liberty of action. These free men
Know how to give their love a certain rough taste, a certain
  clean taste and this liberty
Is the most beautiful reflection there is in the world for it
  recalls to me, it mirrors to me
For it is a reflection of my very own liberty
Which is the secret itself and the mystery
And the centre and the heart and the germ of my Creation.
As I have created man in my image and in my resemblance
So I have created the liberty of man in the image and in the
  resemblance
Of my own, of my original liberty. So when Saint Louis falls on
  his knees

THE MYSTERY OF THE HOLY INNOCENTS

On the flagstones of the Sainte-Chapelle, on the flagstones of
  Notre-Dame
It is a man who falls on his knees, not a thing of rags and
  tatters,
A trembling Oriental slave,
It is a man and a Frenchman, and when Saint Louis loves me
It is a man who loves me and when Saint Louis gives himself
It is a man who gives himself. And when Saint Louis gives me
  his heart
He gives me the heart of a man and the heart of a Frenchman.
  And when he values me at my worth
That is when he values me as God,
It is a man's head which values me, a sound French head.
(And Joinville even, Joinville whom you must not forget.)
When he loves me (for he too loves me),
When he values me (for he too values me),
When he gives himself (for he too gives himself) and when he
  gives me his heart,
He knows what he is, who he is,
He knows what he is worth, he knows what he is weighing, he
  knows what he is giving, he knows what he is bringing
And I know it too.
When Joinville even, and I do not only say Saint Louis,
When Joinville falls on his knees on the flagstones
In the cathedral of Rheims
Or in the simple chapel in his castle at Joinville,
It is not an Oriental slave who is crumpling,
In fear, and in a cowardly and an indecent terror
At the knees and at the feet of some potentate
Of the Orient. But a free man and a French baron,
Joinville, Lord of Joinville,
Who is giving, who is bringing and who is falling on his knees
Freely, and so to say, in a certain sense gratuitously
And a free man and a French baron,

THE HOLY INNOCENTS

Joinville, Lord of Joinville in the County of Champagne,
John, Lord of Joinville, Seneschal of Champagne.

You must not forget Joinville either, God says,
He even dared to answer back to the King.
He even answered back a little to me
With his views on leprosy and mortal sins.
But I let them get away with a great deal, I let them get away
    with as much as they want.

You must not forget Joinville, God says. Those were noble men.
If you forget the sinners, there would not be many left.
A few saints, many sinners, like everywhere else.
But the great procession of sinners is needed
To accompany the few saints. You must also think of the Lord
    of Joinville.

A few saints go ahead. And the great procession of sinners
    follows behind. Of such is my Christendom.
That is how great processions are formed.
A few pastors walk in front. And the great flock follows behind.
    Thus is composed the procession of my Christendom.

As their liberty has been created in the image and in the re-
    semblance of my liberty, God says,
As their liberty is the reflection of my liberty,
So I love to find in them a certain gratuitousness
A reflection of the gratuitousness of my Grace.

THE MYSTERY OF THE HOLY INNOCENTS

Which is as if created in the image and in the resemblance of
the gratuitousness of my Grace.

     *   *   *   *   *   *

To the gratuitousness of my Grace they respond with a certain
gratuitousness of prayer,
And with a certain gratuitousness even in their vows.

They respond to me as I wish. So if it is thus with the humble
people and with a French baron
What must it be with a Saint Louis, a baron himself and King of
the barons.
In their argument about leprosy and mortal sin this is how I
reckon, God says.
When Joinville would rather have committed thirty mortal sins
than be a leper
And when Saint Louis would rather be a leper than commit a
single mortal sin,
I don't consider, God says, that Saint Louis loves me normally
And that Joinville loves me thirty times less than normally,
That Saint Louis loves me according to rule, by the rule,
And that Joinville loves me thirty times less than the rule.
I count the opposite way, God says. This is how I reckon.
This is what I decide.
I decide on the contrary that Joinville loves me normally
Decently as a poor mortal can love me,
Ought to love me.
And that Saint Louis on the contrary loves me thirty times more
than normally,
Thirty times more than decently.
That Joinville loves me according to rule,

THE HOLY INNOCENTS

And that Saint Louis loves me thirty times more than the rule.
(And as for him, if I have put him in my Heaven, at least I know
  the reason why).

That is how I count, God says. And besides, my accounts are
  right. For the leprosy in question,
The leprosy of which they were speaking and of being leprous
Was not an imaginary leprosy and an invented leprosy and a
  theoretical leprosy.
It was not a leprosy they had read of in books and of which they
  had heard tell
More or less vaguely
It was not a leprosy one talked about, or used for frightening
  people with, in conversations and pictures,
But it was a real leprosy and they spoke of really having it
  themselves,
Something they knew well, which they had seen twenty times
In France and in the Holy Land,
That disgusting mealy disease, that filthy plague, that evil scurvy,
That repulsive disease of scabs which makes a man
The horror and the shame of men,
That ulcer, that dry rot, in short that very leprosy
Which eats away the skin and the face and the arm and the hand,
And the thigh and the leg and the foot
And the belly and the skin and the bones and the nerves and the
  veins,
That dry white mould which spreads from place to place
And which nibbles like the teeth of mice,
And which makes a man an outcast and shunned of men,
And which destroys the body like a granular mould
And which breaks out on the body in hideous white lips,
Those hideous dry lips of wounds

THE MYSTERY OF THE HOLY INNOCENTS

And which always advances and never retreats
And which always wins and never loses
And which goes on to the end,
And which makes of a man a walking corpse,
It was of that very leprosy they were speaking, of none other,
It was of that very leprosy they were thinking, of none other,
Of a real leprosy, in nowise of a theoretical leprosy.
It was that very leprosy which he would rather have, none other.
Well I find that I am astonished thirty times over
For it means loving me thirty-fold and thirty-fold of love.

Ah, doubtless if Joinville with the eyes of his soul had seen
What a thing is leprosy of the soul
Which we do not call mortal sin in vain,
If with the eyes of his soul he had seen
That dry rot of the soul infinitely worse,
Infinitely uglier, infinitely more pernicious,
Infinitely more malignant, infinitely more hateful
He would have himself at once understood how absurd was his
   opinion,
And that the question does not even arise. But all do not see
   with the eyes of the soul.
I understand that, God says, all are not saints, such is my
   Christendom.
There are also the sinners, there must be, thus it is.
He was a good Christian, nevertheless, on the whole, though a
   sinner, there must be some in Christendom.
He was a good Frenchman, John Lord of Joinville, one of Saint
   Louis' barons. At least he said what he thought.
Such people make up the bulk of the army. You must have the
   rank and file as well. It is not enough to have leaders who march
   at the head.

THE HOLY INNOCENTS

Such people go very decently to the Crusades, at least once out
of twice and behave very decently on crusade.
They fight very well and get killed very correctly and gain the
Kingdom of Heaven
Like anyone else.
(I mean to say as anyone else would gain the Kingdom of
Heaven.
Or I mean to say as they themselves would gain another kingdom,
A kingdom of earth.) That is what is most remarkable about
them.
They go, one like another, in a flock, one behind the other,
Without hurrying, without surprise, without gesticulating,
Very decently, very ordinarily,
Without making a sensation and they end up all the same
By conquering the kingdom of Heaven.
Or on the other hand they gain the kingdom of Heaven as one
gains a kingdom on earth
With the strong arm and it does not work too badly either.
Violenti rapiunt.
They do that also very decently, very ordinarily, as a matter of
course,
As if it were the most natural thing in the world.
Only these wretched men don't want to have leprosy. They
think no doubt that it is not clean. They would rather have
something else.
The wretches, the fools, if they could see the leprosy of the
soul,
And if they could see the filth or the cleanliness of the soul.
But there, they say to themselves: I have only one body (the
fools they forget the principal thing
They forget not only the soul, but the body of their eternity
The body of the resurrection of the body).

*   *   *   *   *   *

THE MYSTERY OF THE HOLY INNOCENTS

They have the impression that leprosy will annihilate their whole
   body and that it will grip them right to the end (they do not
   consider that at the end of that end begins the veritable
   beginning)
And then they would rather have something else than leprosy.
I think they would rather catch
A disease which would please them. The idea is always the same,
They are willing to face the most terrible trials
And to offer me the most fearful acts of devotion,
Provided that it is they who have previously
Chosen them. Whereupon the Pharisees cry out and make a noise
And utter screams and make grimaces and those execrable Pharisees
Continually pray, saying: Lord, we thank you
That you have not made us like that man
Who is afraid of catching leprosy. Well, as for me I say the
   contrary, God says,
It is I who say: It is no small matter to catch leprosy.
I know what leprosy is. It is I who made it.
I am acquainted with it. I say: It is no small matter to catch
   leprosy.
And I have never said that the trials and the difficulties of their life,
And the diseases and miseries of their life,
And the sorrows of their life were nothing.
On the contrary I have always said and I have always thought
And I have always reckoned that they were something.
And you must in fact believe that they were something
Because my Son did so many miracles for the sick
And because I empowered the King of France
To touch for the King's Evil.

The Pharisees cry out on whoever does not want to catch leprosy
And they are scandalised, those virtuous men.

111

THE HOLY INNOCENTS

But I who am not virtuous,
God says,
I do not cry out and I am not scandalised.

*   *   *   *   *   *

The Pharisees raise an outcry against the man who does not want
    to catch leprosy.
See on the contrary how gently the saint speaks to him,
Firmly but gently.
And that firmness is all the safer and gives me all the more
    certainty and the more assurance and the better guarantee
    because it is gentle.
The hearts of sinners are not taken by force.

They are not pure enough. Only the Kingdom of Heaven is taken
    by force.

The Pharisees hunt down the man who does not want to catch
    leprosy.
See on the contrary how gently the saint reproves him.
At the sinner's words the saint is penetrated by a terrible grief,
But he absorbs, he devours his grief and suffers it himself by
    himself in himself.
And see how gently he reproves the sinner.

And I also, God says, I am on the side of the saints and not at
    all on the side of the Pharisees.

So likewise I absorb and I devour my grief and I suffer it in
   myself by myself,
And see how gently I speak to the sinner
And how gently I reprove the sinner.

And when the brothers were gone,
(He waits till the two brothers whom he had called to him had
   gone away. He waits till they are alone. He does not want to
   give
The appearance of an affront to a French baron),
He called me to him quite alone and made me sit at his feet and said to me :
'Why did you say that to me yesterday?'
And I said to him that I would say it to him again.

          *   *   *   *   *   *

I who never lied to him, it is because Joinville never lied to Saint
   Louis,
Even at the risk of displeasing him, even at the risk of thwarting
   him and causing him heavy grief,
That I am equally certain and I have a guarantee
That Saint Louis never lies to me,
That his love, that his sanctity never lie to me,
That it is in no way a conventional love, a conventional sanctity,
Complacent and imaginary,
But that it is a real sanctity and love,
Frank, of the earth,
Earthly, a sanctity of race and of a fine race,
Free, gratuitous.

And he said to me : 'You speak like a chatterbox

H   *113*

THE HOLY INNOCENTS

(Nothing more, like a chatterbox, a chattering starling):

for you ought to know that no leprosy is so ugly as being in mortal sin, for the soul of him who is in mortal sin resembles the Devil; wherefore no leprosy can be so ugly.

And it is very true that when a man dies he is cured of the leprosy of the body: but when a man dies who has committed a mortal sin, he does not know nor is he certain that he has had in his life such repentance that God has pardoned him; wherefore he should have great fear that his leprosy will endure as long as God shall be in his Paradise. And so I pray you, he said, as strongly as I can, that you will set your heart on this, for the love of God and of me, that you would rather every mischance happened to your body, from leprosy and every disease, than that mortal sin should enter your soul.'

What gentleness, my child, what firmness in gentleness, what
gentleness in firmness.
One and the other bound indissolubly, one forwarding the other,
one setting off the other, one upholding the other, one
nourishing the other.
Gentleness entirely armed with firmness, firmness entirely armed
with gentleness.
One enclosed in the other, the other enclosed in the one, like
a double stone in a double fruit
Of firmness.
A gentleness all the better guaranteed by firmness, a firmness
all the better guaranteed by gentleness.
One bearing the other.

THE MYSTERY OF THE HOLY INNOCENTS

For there is no true gentleness except founded on firmness,
And there is no true firmness except clothed in gentleness.

What gentleness, what tenderness. He who loves
Enters into subjection to him who is loved.
That is how he speaks, he the King of France.
It is true that it is to a French baron,
What care not to offend him,
Not to hurt him in any way, not to injure him,
Not to wound him at all.
Not to leave any trace
Any remembrance of a wound or injury.
What attention, what charity.
What care not to give the least offence.
He the king, speaking for God and for himself
For God and for the King of France he speaks humbly.
He speaks like a trembling petitioner.
It is because in fact he does tremble and he does petition.
He trembles lest that his faithful Joinville should not achieve
   salvation.
And he asks Joinville, he petitions the faithful Joinville
To achieve salvation. To be so good as to achieve his salvation.
   What a petition. He is careful to take him aside. He waits till
   the two brothers are gone.
What gentleness, what father could speak more gently to his son.

     *   *   *   *   *   *

He almost pretends to jest, to begin in a jesting voice *   *
And a profound seriousness comes immediately afterwards
Enters incontinently into the very body and text of that jesting,
That redoubtable introduction. *You speak like a chattering starling.*

THE HOLY INNOCENTS

for you ought to know that no leprosy is so ugly
as being in mortal sin,
for the soul which is in mortal sin resembles the Devil;
wherefore no leprosy can be so ugly.

And the words which follow are not unworthy, my child, of
    the most beautiful words in the Gospels,
Of the grandest words of Jesus in the Gospels. For in imitation
    of Jesus
It has been granted to the Saints to utter words not unworthy
Of Jesus, of the words of Jesus.
As in imitation and in honour of Jesus
It has been granted to the Martyrs to undergo a death
Not unworthy of the death of Jesus. So the words which follow
Are not unworthy of the preaching of Jesus himself.
    And it is very true that when a man dies
he is cured of the leprosy of the body;
(it is the same voice as in the Gospels, my child, the same
    profundity,
the same resonance of the same voice with the same profundity)
(there is also the same sanctity. Jesus and the *other* Saints. The
    same eternal sanctity in common,
The same communion of Saints);
but when a man who has committed a mortal sin dies
he does not know nor is he certain that he has had in his life such repentance
that God has pardoned him:
wherefore he should have great fear that his leprosy will endure
as long as God shall be in Paradise. But the words which follow,
    my child,
Are not unworthy of the heart of the Gospels,
Of the three parables of Hope.
They are a reflection, a carrying forward, a recall,

THE MYSTERY OF THE HOLY INNOCENTS

With the same resonance and in the same line,
As the three parables of Hope. *A man had two sons.* A king had a baron.
A king had a faithful subject. A king had a son. A king had a
   liegeman. And as the three parables of Hope
Are perhaps the heart and certainly the crown of the Gospels
So the words of Saint Louis which follow are perhaps the heart
   and certainly the crown
Not only of Saint Louis and the sanctity of Saint Louis,
But perhaps of all sanctity after the Gospels,
Of all sanctity issuing from the Gospels. For it is a reflection
   and a carrying forward and a recall
Of that unique parable of the son who was lost.

           *   *   *   *   *   *

How should I be less gentle than Saint Louis. Like him I tremble
For their salvation. Like him I petition, alas,
For their salvation. The Pharisees want others to be perfect,
And they insist and they demand. And they talk of nothing else.
   But as for me I am not so exacting.
Because I know what perfection is, I don't ask so much of them.
Because I am perfect and there is none but me who is perfect.
I am the All-Perfect. Therefore I am less particular.

           *   *   *   *   *   *

I find that Joinville is not unworthy and even that he is worthy,
And that it is Saint Louis who is thirty-fold worthy
To be the son of my heart and to lean his shoulder
Against my shoulder.

Moreover what he underwent in Egypt, God says,
And what he caught in Tunis,

117

THE HOLY INNOCENTS

That great exhaustion of all his body
And that incurable
Flux in his bowels of which he died
Was no better than the leprosy he was willing to have.
There is no good disease, God says. I know it, it is I who made
  them.
That is why so many salvations are gained, and the finest, through
  diseases,
And through the worst.
And why so many saints come forth from diseases
As naturally as from their mother's womb and why so much
  saintliness
Issues naturally from the most appalling diseases, the tenderest,
  the dearest, the most flourishing of all saintliness,
And why there is a way of turning disease, and death from disease
  into martyrdom itself.

*   *   *   *   *   *

My son who loved them so much had reason to love them!
  When a man, when the King who has only his body after all
(at least this body on earth and will never have any other on
  earth) (and when he is despoiled of it—by what a spoiling—
  it is once for all)
Says tranquilly that he would rather catch leprosy than fall into
  mortal sin,
That is, he says tranquilly he would rather catch that disease
  than displease me,
Even I cannot get over it, God says, that there should be a man
  like Saint Louis,
(and so many other saints and so many other martyrs)
And I am confounded at being loved so much.

*   *   *   *   *   *

And that he did not utter this sort of enormity,
With a grand gesture, flamboyantly
But that he should have said it simply,
As a matter of course, like an ordinary thing,
In the very thread of his discourse, in the ordinary texture of
  his life,
That is the very flower, God says, that ease,
And in it I recognise the Frenchman
The race to whom everything is simple and common and
  ordinary,
This race of thoroughbreds.

And I recognise here the resonance and the quality of the
  Frenchman
And I salute
Their special character.
People to whom the grandest grandeurs
Are ordinary.
I salute here your liberty, your grace
Your courtesy.

Your graciousness.
Your gratitude.
Your gratuitousness.

Ask a father if his best moment
Is not when his sons begin to love him like men,
Him as a man,
Freely,

THE HOLY INNOCENTS

Gratuitously,
Ask a father whose children are growing up.

       *   *   *   *   *   *

Ask a father if there is not a chosen time above all
And if it is not
Precisely when submission ceases and when his sons become men
Love him (treat him) so to speak from knowledge,
As man to man,
Freely,
Gratuitously. Esteem him thus.
Ask a father if he does not know that nothing is equal
To the glance of a man meeting the glance of a man.

Well, I am their father, God says, and I know man's condition.
It is I who made him.
I do not ask too much of them. I only ask for their hearts.
When I have their hearts, I am satisfied. I am not hard to please.

All the slavish submissions in the world are not worth one frank
    look from a free man.
Or rather all the slavish submissions in the world repel me and
    I would give everything
For one frank look from a free man,
For one beautiful action of obedience and tenderness and de-
    votion from a free man.
For a look from Saint Louis,
And even for a look from Joinville,
For Joinville is less saintly but he is no less free.

THE MYSTERY OF THE HOLY INNOCENTS

(And he is no less a Christian).

And he is no less gratuitous.

And my Son also died for Joinville.
To that liberty, to that gratuitousness I have sacrificed every-
    thing, God says,
To that taste I have for being loved by free men,
Freely,
Gratuitously,
By real men, virile, adult, firm,
Noble, tender but with a firm tenderness.
To obtain that liberty, that gratuitousness I have sacrificed
    everything,
To create that liberty, that gratuitousness,
To set going that liberty, that gratuitousness.

To teach him liberty.

Well, with all my Wisdom I have not too much
To teach him liberty,
With all the Wisdom of my Providence, I have not too much,
And even with the duplicity of my Wisdom for that double
    instruction.
What measures I must observe, and how can I calculate them.
Who else could calculate them. And how double-faced I must be
And how prudently I must arrange that deceit
(This is going to scandalise our Pharisees again),
How prudently I must calculate my very duplicity!
What must not my prudence be! I must create, I must teach
    them liberty

THE HOLY INNOCENTS

Without risking their salvation. For if I support them too much
They will never learn to swim,
But if I do not support them just at the right moment
They go under, they swallow a nasty mouthful, they dive down,
And they must not sink
In that ocean of turpitude.

I am their Father, God says. I am the King, my situation is
    exactly the same,
I am exactly like that king, who was I think a king of England,
Who did not want to send reinforcements, any help
To his son engaged in a desperate battle
Because he wanted the boy
To win his spurs of knighthood himself.
They must win Heaven themselves and they must achieve their
    salvation themselves.
Such is the order, such is the secret, such is the mystery. And
    in this order and in this secret and in this mystery
Our Frenchmen are in the vanguard. They are my chosen
Witnesses.
It is they who advance the furthest alone.
It is they who advance the furthest by themselves.
Above all others they are free and above all others they are
    gratuitous.
They have no need to have the same thing explained twenty times,
Before you have finished speaking, they are off.
Intelligent people,
Before you have finished speaking, they have understood.
Industrious people,
Before you have finished speaking, the work is done.
Military people,
Before you have finished speaking, the battle is fought.

      *   *   *   *   *   *

How annoying, God says. When there are no more Frenchmen,
There are things which I do nobody will any longer understand.

People, the peoples of the earth call you light
Because you are a ready people.
Pharisaical peoples call you light
Because you are a speedy people.
You have arrived before the others have started.
But I have weighed you, God says, and I have in nowise found
   you light.
O people inventors of the Cathedral, I have in nowise found
   you light in faith.
O people inventors of the Crusade I have in nowise found you
   light in charity.
As for hope, we had better not talk of it, there is no one like
   them for that.

Such are our Frenchmen, God says. They are not faultless. Far
   from it. They even have plenty of faults.
They have more faults than others.
But with all their faults, I love them better still than others with
   reputedly fewer faults.
I love them as they are. There is none but I, God says, who is
   faultless. My Son and I. A God and a son.
And as for creatures there are only three who have been faultless,
Not counting the angels.
And those are Adam and Eve before sinning,
And the Virgin temporally and eternally,
In her double eternity.
And only two women have been pure yet of flesh,
And have been of flesh yet pure.
And they are Eve and Mary.

THE HOLY INNOCENTS

Eve before sinning,
Mary eternally.

Our Frenchmen are like everyone, God says,
  Few saints, many sinners   *   *   *
You must take them as they are. If anyone knows it, it is I.
  And besides do you know
How much a single drop of the blood of Jesus
Weighs in my eternal scales?
Then let he who is born for sleeping, sleep. *The earth was without
  form and void; darkness was upon the face of the deep; and the
  Spirit of God moved upon the face of the waters.* And it was only
  afterwards that I created the light. *And God said: Let there be
  light; and there was light.*
*God saw the light that it was good, and God divided the light from
  the darkness.*
*And God called the light day, and the darkness He called night; and
  the evening and the morning were the first day.*
Shall it be said that there will be eyes so extinguished, eyes so
  dimmed
That no spark will ever light them more.
And that there will be voices so exhausted, and souls so dull
That no emotion will ever stir them more.
And that there will be souls so exhausted
By trials, by sorrow,
By tears, by prayer, by toil,
And by having seen what they have seen. And from having
  suffered what they have suffered,
And by having gone through what they have gone through. And
  from knowing what they know.

That they will have had enough of it.
Enough of it for eternity, and all they will ask is to be left
  alone—in peace.

THE MYSTERY OF THE HOLY INNOCENTS

Dona eis, Domine, pacem,
Et requiem aeternam. Peace and eternal rest.
Because they will have learnt certain things about life on earth.
And do not want to hear of anything except a place of rest,
To lie down and sleep in.
To sleep, to sleep at last.
And all that they will be able to bear and all that I can do
And bring
(The man I take in his earthly sleep is fortunate, and it's a good
    sign, my children)
As the desperately ill and the desperately wounded cannot
    endure life any more or the remedy or even the idea of a cure,
But only the balm on the wound.
And no longer have any taste for health.
So shall it be said that on so many wounds,
They will only endure the freshness of balm,
Like a wounded man in a fever.
And that they will no longer have any taste for my Paradise
And for my Eternal Life.
And all that I shall be able to put on so many wounds;
On so many scars and so many sacrifices;
And on the bitterness of so many chalices
And on the thanklessness of so much malice
And on the pricks of so many penances
And on the racked bones of the tortured;

And on the stains of so much blood;

*   *   *   *   *   *

Will be to send down like the balm of evening,
As after the burns of a scorching midday the great descent of a
    fine summer's evening,
The slow fall of an eternal night.

THE HOLY INNOCENTS

O Night, shall it be said I created you last.
And that my Paradise and that my Beatitude
Will be nothing but a great night of clarity,
A great eternal night.
And that the crown of my Judgement and the beginning of
    Paradise and of my Beatitude will be
The sunset of an eternal summer.

And so it would be, God says.
And all I could put on the open mouths
Of the martyrs' wounds
Would be balm and oblivion and night.
And all would finish in lassitude,
That tremendous adventure,
As after a burning harvest
The slow descent of a great summer's evening.
If there were not my little Hope.
For it is through my little Hope alone that Eternity shall be,
And Beatitude shall be,
And Paradise shall be. And Heaven and everything.
For she alone, just as she alone in the days of this Earth
Makes a new morrow spring from an old yesterday.
So from the relics of Judgement Day and from the ruins and the
    rubble of Time
She alone will bring forth new eternity.

I am, God says, the Lord of the Virtues.
Faith is the Sanctuary-lamp,
Which burns eternally.
Charity is that great fire of wood
Which you light on your hearth

So that my children the poor can come and warm themselves
on winter evenings.
And around Faith I see all my faithful
Kneeling together in the same attitudes and with the same voice
And the same prayer.
And around Charity I see all my poor
Sitting in a circle before the fire.
And holding out their palms to the warmth of the hearth.
But my hope is the flower and the fruit and the leaf and the branch
And the sprig and the growth and the germ and the bud.
And she is the growth and the bud and the flower
Of Eternity itself.

         *   *   *   *   *   *

In every family, God says, there is a last-born,
And he is the most cherished.
My little hope who would dance with a skipping-rope in pro-
cessions,
She is in the house of the virtues
As Benjamin was in the house of Jacob.

A man had twelve sons. As the forty-six books of the Old Testament
go before the four Gospels and the Acts and the Apocalypse
Which closes the procession.   *   *   *
And as the battalion of the just goes ahead of the battalion of
Saints.
And Adam ahead of Jesus-Christ
Who is the second Adam.
So ahead of every story and every parable in the New Testament
Goes a story in the Old Testament which is its parallel and its
likeness.

THE HOLY INNOCENTS

A man had two sons. A man had twelve sons.
   And so ahead of every Christian sister
Advances a Jewish sister who is her elder sister and who
   announces her and goes in front,
And who has pitched her tent in the desert. And the well of
   Rebecca
Had been dug before the well of the Samaritan woman.
And above all, one story has pitched its tent,
And before the story of the man who had two sons,
My child, there is the story of the man who had twelve sons.
And as Benjamin was in the family of that man
So is my Hope in the family of the Virtues.
Among the three Theological and the four Cardinal Virtues.
Without counting all the others and notably among those
Among the seven directly opposed to the Capital Sins.
And ahead of the son who was found keeping swine
Goes the son who was found like a king,
I mean to say Minister to a king and in reality Governor of a
   kingdom.
Minister to Pharaoh and Governor of the Kingdom of Egypt.
—I am Joseph, your brother. What Jew, what Christian
Has not wept at that rediscovery.

        *   *   *   *   *   *

A man had twelve sons. So it was, my child,
This was the first time that a child was lost.
This was the first time that a sheep was lost.
This was the first time that a drachma was lost.

But the drachma which had been mislaid,
But the sheep which had strayed,

But the child, that son who had strayed
Was found again on a throne,
Governing the household of Pharaoh
And revictualling the Kingdom of Egypt.
And the one Jesus spoke of, on the contrary (it is always the
    contrary),
The one Jesus spoke of, the lost child of Jesus,
In the parable told by Jesus,
The one Jesus spoke of was found again returning from governing
    a herd of swine.
And I believe that his thirty or forty pigs
Were revictualled with acorns and perhaps with some dirty
    swill,
It is thus, my child. Thus is the Old, thus is the New Testament.
In the Old Testament it is more often a question of thrones.
And in the New Testament it is more often a question of herding
    swine.
(And other animals, who are not less noble).

In the Old Testament there is always a prospect, a thought in
    the direction of commanding.
And in the New Testament, on the contrary, there is always a
    thought,
A secret thought in the direction of service,
And towards servitude.

In the Old Testament there is always a glance, a thought in the
    direction of government.
And in the New Testament there is always a glance, a thought
    in the direction of obedience

THE HOLY INNOCENTS

And towards the simple condition
Towards the simple condition of subjects,
Towards the simple condition of man.

Or if there is a thought in the direction of a command, and of
a government and of a kingdom,
In the New Testament it is in the direction of a command and
of a government and of a kingdom
Which is not at all the government and the command of a
kingdom of Egypt.

And in the New Testament there is no thought but for a kingdom
which is not of this world.

* * * * * *

In the Old Testament there is always a foreboding, there is
always
A sense of fear about a famine of dearth.
In the New Testament there is always a foreboding
Of another unappeasable dearth,
There is always
A sense of fear about a different famine from a different dearth.
For it is a spiritual famine,
From a spiritual dearth.

Thus the Old Testament goes before the New Testament
Thus the histories go before the parables.

And the hymns and the prayers and the psalms
Before the hymns and the prayers and the orisons
And the slow and long line of the Prophets
Before the close battalions,
Before the square battalions
Of the Saints.

Thus the government of the goods of this world proceeds
Before the government of the goods which are not of this world.

Thus the carnal command proceeds
Before the spiritual command.

Thus the temporal kingdom
Proceeds before the eternal kingdom.

* * * * * *

All the Old Testament is a figure, an image, very faithful, very
 exact
In the mass and in detail,
(But faithfully inverse, exactly inverse),
Of the New Testament in the mass and in its detail.
In the Old Testament the creation is on the threshold,
At the beginning which is the beginning of the world.
And in the New Testament the judgement is at the end,
The judgement which is strictly the opposite of the Creation.
The other end, which is strictly a counter-creation.

THE HOLY INNOCENTS

For at the Creation I made the world,
(The temporal world)
And at the judgement I unmake it.
Thus the judgement is strictly the opposite and the counter-
weight to the creation:
That which can be put against, that which counterbalances the
creation.

I have carved time out of eternity, God says,
Time and the world of time.
The Creation was the beginning and the Judgement will be the
end.
(Of time) (Of the world of time).
It is exactly symmetrical, balanced.
What I have opened, I shall close.
On the day of Creation (the six days) I opened a certain world
(It is well known for that matter)
(It is well known, it has been sufficiently talked about)
In short at the first hour of the first of the six days of creation
I began a certain story,
And on the Day of Judgement I shall close it.
And all the Old Testament starts with a judgement, a decision
I made to create.
And all the New Testament goes towards a judgement, a decision
I shall make to judge.
Thus the Old Testament is symmetrical with the New,
And (counter-)balances the New.
And all the Old Testament starts from that Creation.
And all the New Testament goes towards that Judgement.
And in the Old Testament Paradise is at the beginning.
And it is an earthly Paradise.
But in the New Testament Paradise is at the end.

THE MYSTERY OF THE HOLY INNOCENTS

And I tell you that it is a celestial
Paradise.
And all the Old Testament goes towards John the Baptist and
  towards Jesus.
But all the New Testament comes from Jesus.
It is like a great arch which rises from two sides towards the
  keystone
And Jesus is the keystone. Such is the arch of that nave.
And the stone which rises following the curve of the nave,
Deciding, designing in advance and proportionately the curve
  of the nave,
Forming the curve of the arch,
The stone which rises from the base comes upward boldly,
And faithfully and surely,
In all security, without any disquiet,
Because in rising it knows very well
That it will find the keystone punctual at the rendez-vous,
At the exact intersection, at the sacred crossing, and that the
  keystone is Jesus.
And all the arch together upholds and carries and raises and
  supports the keystone
Like an enormous round, neckless shoulder supporting a single
  head, but the keystone alone,
The keystone which is completion,
Alone likewise entirely upholds the arch and everything.
And the last stone before the keystone is John the Baptist.
But the first stone after the keystone is Peter the Founder.
Thou art Peter and on this rock.
And he was crucified head downwards,
That is to say, redescending.
And the stone being quadrangular
There are four angles and four lines to the square.
And we say, *according to Matthew, according to Mark, according to
  Luke, according to John.*

THE HOLY INNOCENTS

That is *following the line of Matthew, following the line of Mark,*
   following the line of Luke,
And *following the line of John.*
And at the four corners are seated the young man, the lion, the
   bull and the eagle.
For the Church is quadrangular,
As she is lapidary being founded on the quadrangular
Rock.

　　　*　　　*　　　*　　　*　　　*　　　*

And the keystone of this mystic arch,
The keystone itself
Carnal, spiritual,
Temporal, eternal,
Is Jesus,
Man,
God.

And the creation was in a way an opening of time and in a way
   a closing of eternity.
And the judgement will be strictly the closing of time
And the total and definitive
Reopening of eternity.

　　　*　　　*　　　*　　　*　　　*　　　*

You send children to school, God says.
I think it is to forget the little they know.
It would be better to send the parents to school.
It is they who have need of it.

But naturally it would have to be a school of mine,
And not a school of men.

You believe that children know nothing.
And that parents and grown-up people know something.
Well, I tell you it is the contrary.
(It is always the contrary).
It is the parents, it is the grown-up people who know nothing.
And it is the children who know
Everything.

For they know first innocence,
Which is everything.

The world is always inside out, God says.
And in the contrary sense.
Happy is he who remains like a child
And who like a child keeps
His first innocence.

My Son said it to them often enough,
Without any evasion and without any mitigation.
For he spoke distinct and strong.
And clear.
Happy, not even, not only he
Who is like a child, who remains like a child.
But truly happy is the man who is a child, who remains a child,

THE HOLY INNOCENTS

Strictly, precisely the child that he himself was.
Because truly it has been granted to every man
To be.
Because it is granted to every man to have been
A young, milky child.

Because every man has been granted that benediction,
That unique grace.

And the kingdom of heaven is not at a lower price,
At another price.
My Son said it to them often enough.
And in quite explicit terms.

The Kingdom of Heaven will only be for them.
And there will be nothing except for them.
*At the same time the disciples came unto Jesus, saying, who is the
greatest in the Kingdom of Heaven?*

*And Jesus called a little child unto Him, and set him in the midst of
them.*

*And said: Verily I say unto you, except ye be converted, and become as
little children, ye shall not enter into the Kingdom of Heaven.*

*Whosoever therefore shall humble himself as this little child, the same is
greatest in the Kingdom of Heaven.*

THE MYSTERY OF THE HOLY INNOCENTS

And whosoever shall receive one such little child in My name receiveth me.

But whosoever shall offend one of these little ones who believe in me, it were better for him that a millstone were hanged about his neck and that he were drowned in the depths of the sea.

You have schools, God says. I think it is in order to unlearn
The little that you know.
Life also is a school, they say. You learn something every day.
I know that life which begins at Baptism and ends at Extreme
Unction.
It is a perpetual wearing away, a continual spreading decay.
One is always going downwards.
Happy is he who remains as he was on the day of his Baptism
And of his first Communion. Life begins at Baptism, God says,
Shall it be said that it ends at the first,
And not in fact at the last Communion.
Shall it be said that a man ends with his first Communion.
And not in fact with the Viaticum, which is his last Communion.

They cram themselves full of experience, they say; they gain
experience; they learn about life; from day to day they
accumulate experience. A singular treasure, God says.
Treasure of emptiness and want.
Treasure of the seven years' famine, treasure of emptiness and
withering and of growing old.
Treasure of wrinkles and anxieties.
Treasure of the lean years. Increase that treasure, God says. In
empty granaries

137

THE HOLY INNOCENTS

You heap up the empty sacks
Of an empty Egypt.
You increase the treasure of your troubles and your miseries.
And the sacks of your cares and your pettiness.
You acquire experience, you say, you increase your experience.
You are always going downwards, God says, you are always
    growing less, you are always losing.
You are always going downhill. You are always growing withered
    and wrinkled and older.
And you will never climb up the hill again.
As for what you call experience, your experience, I call it waste,
    diminution, decrease, the loss of hope.

And I call it a pretentious wasting,
The diminution, the decrease, the loss of innocence.

And a perpetual degradation.

For it is innocence which is full and experience which is empty.
It is innocence which wins and experience which loses.

It is innocence which is young and experience which is old.
It is innocence which grows and experience which shrinks.

It is innocence which is born and experience which dies.
It is innocence which knows and experience which does not
    know.

It is the child who is full and the man who is empty.

THE MYSTERY OF THE HOLY INNOCENTS

Empty like an empty pumpkin and like an empty barrel.

There, God says, that is what I think of your experience.

Go, my children, go to school.
And you, men, go to the school of life.
Go to learn
To unlearn.

     *   *   *   *   *   *

Nothing is so beautiful as a child who falls asleep while saying
its prayers, God says.
I tell you there is nothing so beautiful in the world.
I have never seen anything so beautiful in the world.
And yet I have seen some beauty in the world
And I am a judge of it. My Creation overflows with beauty.
My Creation overflows with marvels.
There are so many one doesn't know where to put them.
I have seen millions and millions of stars rolling at my feet like
the sands of the sea.
I have seen days blazing like flames.
Summer days in June, in July, in August.
I have seen winter evenings laid down like a cloak.
I have seen summer evenings as calm and gentle as the descent
of Paradise
All sprinkled with stars.
I have seen the slopes of the Meuse and the churches which are
my own houses.
And Paris and Rheims and Rouen and the cathedrals which are
my own palaces and my own castles.

THE HOLY INNOCENTS

So beautiful that I shall keep them in Heaven.
I have seen the capital of the kingdom and Rome the capital of
    Christendom.
I have heard the singing of Mass and of triumphant Vespers.
And I have seen those plains and valleys of France
Which are more beautiful than anything.
I have seen the dark, deep sea, and the dark, deep forest, and
    the dark, deep heart of man.
I have seen hearts devoured by love
Throughout a life-time
Lost in charity.
Burning like flames.
I have seen martyrs inspired by faith
Holding firm as a rock on the torturer's frame
Between the iron teeth.
(Like a soldier holding firm all alone all his life
Through faith
In his General [apparently] absent).
I have seen martyrs flaming like torches
Earning palms forever green,
And I have seen gathering beneath the iron claws
Drops of blood which glittered like diamonds.
And I have seen the dropping of many tears of love
Which will endure longer than the stars of the sky.
And I have seen faces of prayer, faces of tenderness
Lost in charity.
Which will shine eternally through endless nights.
And I have seen whole lives from birth to death,
From baptism to the Viaticum,
Unroll like a fair skein of wool.
Well, I tell you, God says, I know nothing so beautiful in all
    the world
As a little child who falls asleep while saying his prayers
Under the wing of his Guardian Angel

And who laughs to the angels as he goes to sleep.

And who is already confusing everything and understanding
nothing more

And who stuffs the words of the *Our Father* all awry, pell-mell
into the words of the *Hail Mary*

While a veil is already dropping on his eyelids

The veil of night on his face and his voice.

I have seen the greatest Saints, God says. Yet I say to you.

I have never seen anything so funny and in consequence I know
nothing so beautiful in the world

As the child who falls asleep saying his prayers

(As the little creature who falls asleep confidently)

And who jumbles his *Our Father* with his *Hail Mary*.

Nothing is so beautiful and it is even a point

On which the Blessed Virgin is of my opinion

About it.

And I can truly say it is the only point on which we are of the
same opinion. For generally we are of contrary opinions.

Because she is in favour of mercy,

While it is necessary that I should be in favour of justice.

      *   *   *   *   *   *

As for you men (God says), just try to invent a child's saying.

You know very well that you cannot.

And not only that you cannot invent one

Not even one, but when they are uttered

You cannot even remember them. When a child's saying breaks
forth among you

You cry out, you break forth yourselves in a wonder

Which is sincere and profound and which will redeem you and
to which I do justice.

And you say, the whole of you says,

You say with your eyes, you say with your voice,

THE HOLY INNOCENTS

You laugh, you say to yourselves and you say aloud at the table:
That's good, that is, I must remember it. And you swear to
  yourselves
To share it with your friends, to tell it to everybody,
You have so much pride in your children (I don't blame you
  for it, God says,
It is what is best in you and it is what will redeem you).
You think that you can easily relate it.
But when all afire you begin to relate it,
You realise that you no longer remember it.
And not only that, but you cannot find it again. It has vanished
  from your memory.
It is too pure a water and has fled from your muddy memory,
  your stained memory.
And it wanted to flee, it did not want to remain.

*　　*　　*　　*　　*　　*

And you feel truly that it is so, that it is just, and that nothing
  will return and that nothing can be done about it,
And that it is your former soul,
O men,
That has passed by.

*　　*　　*　　*　　*　　*

When a child's saying is uttered in the family circle,
When a child's saying
Falls
Among the confusion of the day,
Among the noise of the day,
(In the sudden silence),
In the sudden recollection
At the family table.

142

THE MYSTERY OF THE HOLY INNOCENTS

O men and women seated at that table suddenly bowing your
   heads, you listen to the passing-by
Of your former soul.

*   *   *   *   *   *

A voice has come,
Men at table,
As if from another creation.

A voice has risen,
Men at table,
A voice has come,
It is from a world where you once were.

A spring has gushed,
Men at table,
It is the spring of your first soul.
You also have spoken thus.

You were other men, men at table.
You were other beings, men at table.
You were children like them.

You uttered children's sayings, men at table.
Only try nowadays to utter children's sayings.

A saying has passed, a saying has risen, a saying has come, men
   at table.
A saying has fallen in the silence of your table.

THE HOLY INNOCENTS

And suddenly you have recognised,
And suddenly you have saluted,
Your former soul.

* * * * * *

Sinite parvulos venire ad me.
Talium est enim regnum coelorum are the words of my Son.
But they are not only the words of my Son. They are my words.
What a pledge, and the Church, my daughter the Church makes
me repeat them
And makes me say them (and I shall never disavow a liturgy,
A prayer, an address of my daughter the Church).
Through the Church, through the ministry of the Priest I have
repeated the pledge, I have repeated the words of my Son:
Suffer the little ones to come unto me.
For of such is the Kingdom of Heaven.
Thus is my Roman liturgy entwined with my central and cardinal
teaching
And with my Jewish prophecies.
And the chain is Jewish and Roman, passing through a hinge, an
articulation,
Through a central origin.
Everything is foretold in my Jewish prophecies.
At the centre, at the heart, everything is realised, everything is
consummated by my Son.
Everything is consummated, everything is celebrated by my
Roman liturgy.

The Jewish prophet foretells it.
My Son tells it.
And I retell it.

And it is retold for me.

THE MYSTERY OF THE HOLY INNOCENTS

And there is a recall, an echo, a reminder and as it were a return,
which is Saint Louis.
I mean: There is a recall, an echo, a reminder and as it were a
return which are the Saints.

There is a reflection.

There is a light beforehand, a light during, a light, a reflection
afterwards.

There have been three journeys into Egypt, God says. And once
it is Joseph.
And once it is Jesus.
And once it is Saint Louis.

There have been three journeys into Egypt and it is a strange
land.

And once it was Joseph leading Jacob, that is Israel.
And once it was Joseph leading Jesus.
And once it was Saint Louis leading Joinville
And the lesser people of France and the other French barons.

Strange Egypt, God says, singular destiny of this temporal Egypt.
High and triple destiny. Three journeys were made.
A flight. A flight. A crusade.
An entry. A retreat. A crusade.
A child sold. A child in flight. A king on crusade.

K   *145*

THE HOLY INNOCENTS

A minister of the king. A king on an ass. A king in prison.
O stage of Egypt. Three times they played on it.

Once beforehand. Once during. Once afterwards.

      *   *   *   *   *   *

Ancient land, land of Egypt, thou seemest asleep, but thy sleep
   has been troubled three times
By footsteps which have come.

Land, thou hast been blessed three times and thou, barren desert,
   hast been watered three times,
Rorate, coeli, desuper. Et nubes pluant justum.
Heavens, drop your dew from on high. And may the clouds water the Just.

Heavens, drop your dew. O land of Egypt, God says, mysterious
   land.
Thou hast furnished a mysterious history,
Thou hast furnished a mysterious destiny,
Thou hast been greatly honoured in temporal things,
Sleeping land three times awakened,
Unknown land three times visited,
Forgotten land three times remembered.

Thus, God says, everything is acted three times. The Prophet
   speaks beforehand.

THE MYSTERY OF THE HOLY INNOCENTS

My Son speaks during.
The Saint speaks afterwards.

And I speak now and ever.

And thus you see that my Son is the centre and the heart and
  the arch and the keystone
And the vault and the cross of the axis,
The point of articulation.
The hinge on which the door turns,
The Prince of the prophets and the Prince of the Saints.

The Prophet, the just man, comes beforehand.
My Son comes during.
The Saint comes afterwards.

As for me I come now and ever.

And the Church which is the communion of Saints and the
  communion of the faithful likewise comes afterwards, like-
  wise comes now and ever.

And I shall not allow my Church to fall short, God says, I shall
  not allow her to err, I shall not allow her to fail.
Ancient land of Egypt who seemest asleep, who really art
  watching,
I am as truly pledged by the commandments of my Son as by my
  own
Commandments.
I am as truly pledged by the teaching of the Church as by my own
Teaching.

THE HOLY INNOCENTS

I am as truly pledged by a liturgy as I was pledged to Moses
And as my Son pledged himself to those on the Mount.
And that, which my Son said once, *sinite parvulos venire ad me*—
    suffer the little ones to come unto me—I repeat it, it is repeated
    for me every time (what a pledge).
And my Son said it of a few children who were playing, and who,
    once blessed, left him to return to their game,
But as for me, I say it, it is said for me to every child who will
    never return to play
Except in my Paradise.

Yes, those words (what a pledge) I repeat at the Office for the
    Dead in which everything ends,
Towards which everything leads. *Office of the Dead for the Burial
    of a Child.*

*   *   *   *   *   *

The celebrant chants
The old Psalm of King David
Beati immaculata in via.
Blessed are the undefiled in the way.

Blessed are the undefiled in the way.
Beati immaculata in via.
Shall it be said, God says, that of so many saints and of so many
    martyrs
The only ones who will be really white
Really pure,
The only ones who will be really without stain will be
Those unfortunate children whom the soldiers of Herod

148

THE MYSTERY OF THE HOLY INNOCENTS

Massacred in their mother's arms.

O Holy Innocents, will you then be the only ones.

Holy Innocents, will you then be the pure ones.

Holy Innocents, will you then be the white and stainless ones.

Beati immaculata in via.

Blessed are the innocent, the stainless in the way.

Ego sum via, veritas et vita.

I am the Way, the Truth and the Life.

O Holy Innocents, shall it be said that you will be and that you
are

The only innocents?

And that beside you even Francis, my servant, is not poor?

And that beside you my servant Saint Louis of France

Is not innocent?

Shall it be said there is in life, and in existence on this earth, so
much bitterness, so much lassitude,

So much thanklessness.

So much blight.

So much mist.

Such an irrevocable aging of the soul and of the body.

Such a stain, such ineffaceable wrinkles.

A dullness which can never more be quickened.

A fever which can never more be cooled.

A downward slope which can never more be reascended.

A furrow of memory, of inability to forget.

Such a depth, such a furrow of pain at the corners of the mouth

That the greatest sanctities in the world will never efface that
furrow.

And that the greatest sanctities in the world will never be worth

The mouths without lines, the souls without memory,

The bodies without scar

Of those very great saints and very great martyrs who only left
their mothers' breasts

To enter into the Kingdom of Heaven.

THE HOLY INNOCENTS

And who knew nothing of life and received from life no wound
Except that wound which gave them entry into the Kingdom of
   Heaven.
The only Christians assuredly who on Earth had never heard tell
   of Herod?
And to whom, on Earth, the name of Herod meant nothing
   at all.
Shall it be said that the greatest sanctities in the world
Whole lives of sanctity
Will not have unfurrowed will not have unwrinkled the soul.
And that even the rack will not have gained for the martyrs
A certain whiteness, a certain freshness,
A certain integrity
Belonging to earliest
Innocent childhood?
And that what is regained, defended inch by inch, retaken,
   gained,
Is in no way the same as what has never been lost?
And that a bleached paper is in no way a white paper?
And that a bleached fabric is in no way a white material?
And that a bleached soul is in no way a white soul?
And that the nearest to me will be those white milky children
Who never knew anything of life and did nothing in existence
Except receive a good sabre cut.
I mean to say struck at the right moment?

*   *   *   *   *   *

I looked, John says,
*I looked and lo, a Lamb stood on the mount Sion, and with him an
   hundred and forty and four thousand, having his name and his
   Father's name written on their foreheads. And I heard a voice from
   Heaven as the voice of many waters and as the voice of a great
   thunder; and I heard the voice of harpers harping with their harps.*

THE MYSTERY OF THE HOLY INNOCENTS

And they sang
quasi canticum novum,

as it were a new song before the throne,

and before the four beasts and before the elders;

et nemo poterat dicere canticum,

and no man could learn that song,

nisi illa centum quadraginta quatuor millia,

but the hundred and forty and four thousand,

qui empti sunt de terra,

who were taken away,

who have been taken away from the Earth,

You understand, my child, *qui empti sunt de terra, who have been
  taken away from the Earth.* Everybody is taken away from the
  Earth, on his day, at his hour.
But everybody is taken away from the Earth too late, when
  already the Earth has taken hold of him.
Everybody is taken away from the Earth when he is already earthy,

When his memory is earthy and when his soul is earthy.
When the earth has stuck to him and when it has left on him
An ineffaceable mark.
But they, they alone *empti sunt de terra*, literally *they were taken
away from the Earth*
Before they had in any way become involved in the Earth.
Before the Earth had given them, had left on them
The least earthy mark.
Empti sunt de terra. The Earth did not take hold of them at all,
did not have them at all. The Earth had no power over them.
Did not nourish them at all. Did not print on them in any way
that imprint,
That indelible mark.
They were taken away from the earth, that is to say from earthy
ingratitude,
And earthly bitterness and earthly aging.
They were taken away from the earth, not after having been there
like us, like everybody.
But *they were taken away from the earth*, that is from being there
at all.
From being there and from eternally having been there.
Shall it be said, God says, that all the grandeurs of the Earth
and even the blood of the martyrs
Are not worth as much as not having been of the Earth?
As not having an earthy flavour?
As having been *taken away* at the beginning,
At the start, at the starting point of this earthly life?
As not having those furrows and that flavour of an earthy
Disappointment,
And bitterness?

Beati ac sancti. Blessed and holy these Holy
Innocents. *These are*, John says,

THE MYSTERY OF THE HOLY INNOCENTS

These are they which follow the Lamb wherever he goes,

Hi sequuntur Agnum quocumque ierit.

Hi empti sunt. Again. *Empti sunt. Were taken away.*

Hi empti sunt ex hominibus,

These were taken away from among men,

primitiae Deo, et Agno :

first-fruits unto God and to the Lamb ;

et in ore eorum non est inventum mendacium ;

and in their mouth,
and on their lips was found no falsehood ;

(The falsehood of men, the adult falsehood, the earthly falsehood,
The earthy falsehood).

sine macula enim sunt ante thronum Dei.

for they are without stain before the throne of God.

Such is, God says, the secret of tenderness and of grace
Which is in childhood itself, at its starting point.
Such is the innocence, the whiteness, the freshness.
Such is the secret, the favour of my Grace,
(The unjustifiable justice),
That there are those who are imbrued in the Earth and those who
    are not imbrued in the Earth.

THE HOLY INNOCENTS

Those who are marked, stained, spattered by the Earth and those
who are not spattered by the Earth.

And there is something only for those who are not imbrued in
the Earth and who are not spattered by the Earth.

It is they, the Apostle says, who on Mount Sion stand around the
Lamb.

They are a hundred and forty and four thousand and it is they
who have

My name and the name of my Son on their foreheads.

And the Apostle heard a voice from heaven.

Like the voice of many waters.

And like the voice of a great thunder.

And like the voice of harpers, harping with their harps.

And, notice, they did not only sing a song.

But they sang as it were a *new* song before the throne.

And before the four beasts, and the elders;

It is a *new* song to mark

The eternal newness that there is in childhood.

And which is the great secret of my grace.

This recurring, this perpetually recurring, this eternally recurring
newness.

And the new song comes from the newness itself. Issues from
it. Is born of it.

Well, this is their privilege. And there is not any greater.

       *   *   *   *   *   *

To so many others. To all those other witnesses, to all those
other martyrs, it was not granted.

Eternally it was not granted to sing a new song.

Such is my rule, such is the secret of my hierarchy.

A whole life of training and of prayer.

A life of trials, a life of humility does not suffice.

A life of merits, a life of virtue is no help at all.

A life of blood, a life of tears, even a life of grace has nothing
to do with it.

For what is needed precisely is a life which is not whole.

Which is the least lived, which is hardly begun.

Which is the least possible begun. *Et nemo poterat dicere canticum.*
And those hundred and forty and four thousand

Who alone could sing that new song, what had they done?

Wonder now at the order of my Grace. They had done this,

They had come into the world. One thing, that is all, or to put
it otherwise,

They had done this, to have been little new-born babies.

They were a group of little Jewish sucklings.

Boys and girls.

Their mothers said as in all countries in the world: *Mine is the
prettiest.*

As for them, being pretty mattered nothing to them. Provided
they could sleep and suck,

When they were drowsy.

When they wanted to sleep they slept;

When they were hungry and thirsty (together)

When they wanted to suck, they sucked;

When they wanted to cry they cried;

Those were their greatest occupations. It was thus that they
found

Not only the Kingdom of God and Eternal Life,

But they alone have written on their foreheads my Name and
the Name of my Son.

And they alone sing there a new song.

* * * * * *

. . . Well, if we have made of them what you see, God
says,

There are seven reasons for it which I will gladly tell you.

155

THE HOLY INNOCENTS

The first is that I love them, God says, and that is enough.
Such is the hierarchy of my Grace.

The second is that they please me, God says, and that is enough.
Such is the hierarchy of my Grace.

The third is that it pleases me thus, God says, and that is enough.
Such is the hierarchy, such is the order, such is the ordinance
    of my Grace.

Now I am going to tell you, God says, the fourth,
And it is precisely because they have no lines at the corners of
    their mouths,
Lines of disappointment and of bitterness, injuries of Time,
Those lines of experience, those lines of memory which we see
    on every mouth.

The fifth, God says, is that by a sort of exchange,
By a sort of equipoise those Innocents paid for my Son,
While they were lying on the stones of the roads, on the stones
    of the towns, on the stones of the villages
In the dust and in the mud, less esteemed than lambs and kids
    and piglets
(For lambs and kids and piglets are highly esteemed by the
    butcher and by the consumer)
Abandoned on the bodies of their mothers
During that time my Son was fleeing. It must be said.
It was a willed misunderstanding,
Which is serious. It must be said.
They were taken for him. They were massacred for him. In his
    stead. In his place.

THE MYSTERY OF THE HOLY INNOCENTS

Not only because of him, but for him, counting as him.

Representing him so to say. Being substituted for him. Resembling him. Almost being (another) him.

In representation, in substitution, in replacement of him. Well, all that is serious, God says, all that counts. They were like my Son and replaced him.

Exactly when the question was nothing less

When the intention was nothing less than of murdering him,

(Prematurely, before he was ready),

When Herod wanted to murder him. All that must be paid for, God says.

And because they were found to resemble my Son at the exact moment of that massacre,

That is why at present they are found to resemble the Lamb in his eternal glory.

During that time led by a second Joseph

My Son was fleeing towards ancient Egypt. They acquired thus. These urchins, these less than urchins procured thus.

A credit with us. Riding on an ass with his Mother

(As thirty years later, riding on the foal of an ass

He would enter Jerusalem),

Thirty years earlier riding on an ass with his Mother, my Son

Retraced the journey of the patriarch Jacob. And those infants gained in the mêlée.

In their own ranks those sucklings gained

A credit with me. They were quite right.

Blessed are they who have a credit with us. We are very good debtors.

The sixth reason, God says, (I think it is the sixth) (it is a very good investment to be taken for my Son and which pays well),

157

THE HOLY INNOCENTS

The sixth reason is that they were the contemporaries of my
   Son.
The same age and born at the same time,
Just at that moment of time.
We too favour our comrades in the annual levy.
Such is the prize we have given to Time.
It is a great chance or a great mischance for every man
To be born or not to be born at a certain moment of Time.
It is a chance or a mischance over which nothing prevails.
Which you cannot reverse, which nothing can reverse.
And one of the greatest mysteries of Grace is the share of chance,
That irrevocable, indefectible share
Which we have left to the benefits of chance as opposed to the
   benefits which are not of chance;
To the flesh as opposed to and within the spirit;
To the temporal as opposed to and within the eternal, that is
   to say
To matter in the creation, and to the creature, and to the
   creation and even to the matter of the creation as opposed
   to the Creator.

To such a point, God says, that we ourselves are not indifferent
   to dates; to Time;
To the influence of dates and that we secretly love those hundred
   and forty and four thousand
because they found themselves there and we love them
   with a secret unique love
because they found themselves born there, because they were,
because they found themselves to be
Of the same age as my Son, born at the same time, of the same
   race.
At the same date.

In short because together they made a levy.
Not only a levy of Jews but a levy of men
(Such was the new Law)
The levy of Jesus Christ.
And undeniably they were
(time has always a certain weight, always bears a certain un-
deniable evidence)
Undeniably they were
His comrades in the annual levy.
(There is always in time, in a date
Something which is irrefutable).

The seventh reason, God says, why conceal it? It is that they
were similar to my Son.
And he was similar to them.
(A generation of men, God says,
an annual levy is like a beautiful long wave
which advancing from end to end on an even front
with a single sweep on an even front from end to end
breaks all at once on the shore of the sea.
Thus a generation, an annual levy is a wave of men.
Advancing all together on an even front,
and all together on an even front crashing down like a wall of
water
when it reaches the Eternal shore).
My Son was soft like them and like them he was new.
He was more or less unknown. Like them.
That mighty double adoration which (without it) had already
put him above comparison.
The mighty double adoration of the Shepherds and the Magi was
already half-forgotten.
He had become quite unknown again. And the Magi had made a
fool of Herod.

THE HOLY INNOCENTS

He was not two years old, he was like them.
He was a beautiful child, his Mother said so.

He did not yet suspect
The ingratitude of man.

He did not have as yet at the corners of his mouth
The lines of bitterness and disappointment.

He had not yet at the corners of his eyes
The wrinkles, the lines of tears and of having seen too much.

He had not yet in the corners of his memory
The lines engraved by the impossibility of forgetting.

He did not yet know, as man he did not know any vicissitudes.
He did not know, as man he did not know what was going to
    leave an eternal mark.
the crown of thorns and the sceptre of reed.
and the hideous agony of Calvary.
and the even more hideous agony of the vigil at night
on the Mount of Olives.
Like them he was an alabaster vase
Which no mark had yet stained,
No dregs of any scum.
And this is the sixth reason, God says, and the seventh. They
    remind me of my Son.
As he would have been if he had not changed since then, as he
    was when he was so beautiful. If that stupendous adventure
Had stopped there. That is why I love them, God says, above
    all others they are witnesses of my Son.
They show me, they are as he was, if only
He had never changed. Of all the imitations of Jesus Christ

THE MYSTERY OF THE HOLY INNOCENTS

Theirs is the first and it is the freshest; and it is the only one
Which is not in any degree
Which is not even a fraction
Of an imitation of some brand and some bruise and some wound in the heart of Jesus.
Theirs is a total ignorance of outrage and affronts,
And of injuries and insults.
They are only aware of murder, and of having been killed, which is nothing.
They were never turned to derision.
That is what I love in them, God says. That is why, for what I love them.
They are for me children who have never become men.
Lambs who have never become rams.
Or sheep. (*And these follow the Lamb wherever he goes*).
Infant Christs who will never grow old. Who never grew up.
    While *mine grew*
in wisdom, and in age and in grace
and in favour with God and man.

I love them innocently, God says. And that is the seventh reason.
(It is thus you must love innocents).
As the father of a family loves his son's friends
Who go to school with him.

But as for them they have not moved since that far-off time.

They are the eternal imitations
Of what Jesus was during a very short time

THE HOLY INNOCENTS

For he *grew*, indeed. He grew up
For that enormous adventure.

*   *   *   *   *   *

And the Apostle calls them *primitiae Deo et Agno: first-fruits unto
God and to the Lamb.* That is to say the first-fruits of the earth
which you offer to God and to the Lamb. The other Saints are
the ordinary fruits, the fruits in season. But they are the fruits
Of the very promise of the season.

And following the Apostle the Church repeats: *Innocentes pro Christo
infantes occisi sunt,*

*the Innocents for Christ
were massacred while infants,*

*   *   *   *   *   *

*ipsum sequuntur Agnum sine macula
they follow the Lamb himself without stain*

(and the text is such, my child, that it is both the Lamb who is
without stain
and they with him who are without stain).

But the Church goes further, the Church goes beyond, the
Church goes beyond the Apostle.

The Church does not only say they are first-fruits to God and
to the Lamb,
The Church invokes them and names them

162

THE MYSTERY OF THE HOLY INNOCENTS

flowers of the Martyrs

Thus meaning literally that the *other* Martyrs are the fruits but
that these, among the Martyrs, are the flowers themselves.

Salvete FLORES *Martyrum,*

Hail FLOWERS *of the Martyrs.*

Stretched on the rack, tied to the rack like fruit tied to espaliers
The other martyrs, twenty centuries of martyrs
Centuries and centuries of martyrs
Are literally fruits in season,
In every season spread on espaliers
And chiefly fruits of autumn
And my Son even was gathered
In his thirty-third season. But they, those simple innocents
They are even before the fruit, they are the promise of fruit.
Salvete flores Martyrum, those children of less than two years old
    are the flowers of the other Martyrs.
That is, the flowers which produce the other martyrs.
At the very beginning of April they are the pink flowers of the
    peach-tree.
In the middle of April, at the very beginning of May they are
    the white flowers of the pear-tree.
In the middle of May they are the red flowers of the apple-tree.
White and red.
They are the flower itself and the bud of the flower and the down
    on the bud.
They are the burgeoning of the branch and the burgeoning of
    the flower.
They are the glory of April and they are sweet hope.
They are the glory of the woods and of the months.
They are early childhood.

THE HOLY INNOCENTS

Reminiscere Sunday is all for them, because they remember.
Oculi Sunday is all for them, because they see.
Laetare Sunday is all for them, because they rejoice.
Passion Sunday is all for them, because they were the first Passion.
Palm Sunday is all for them, because they were the palm branches
    which have borne so much fruit.
And Easter Sunday is all for them, because they are risen.
They are the blossom of the hawthorn which flowers in Holy Week,
And the blossom of the forerunner, the blackthorn, which
    flowers five weeks earlier.
They are the flowers of all rosaceous plants and trees,
Promise of so many martyrs they are the rose-buds
Of blood-bedewed roses.
Salvete flores Martyrum,
Hail flowers of the Martyrs,

quos lucis ipso in limine,
Christi insecutor sustulit,

ceu turbo nascentes rosas.

who on the very threshold of light,
the persecutor of Christ swept away,
(carried off)

ceu turbo nascentes rosas.

as a tempest the budding roses.
(that is, as the tempest, as a tempest **sweeps off, carries away**
    the budding roses).

Vos prima Christi victima,
Grex immolatorum tener,

THE MYSTERY OF THE HOLY INNOCENTS

Aram sub ipsam simplices
Palma et coronis luditis.

You, first victims for Christ,
Infant flock of sacrifices,
Even on the steps of the altar, simple ones
(Simplices, simple souls, simple children),
Palma et coronis luditis. You play with the palms and crowns. With
  your palms and crowns.

Such is my Paradise, God says. My Paradise could not be simpler.
Nothing is less elaborate than my Paradise.
Aram sub ipsam, on the steps of the altar itself
These simple children *play* with their palms and their martyrs'
  crowns,
That is what is going on in my Paradise. Whatever can they
  play at
With palms and martyrs' crowns.
I believe they play at hoops, God says, and perhaps at quoits
(at least I believe so, for do not think
that they ever ask my permission)
And the palm forever green they use apparently as a hoop-stick.

BIOGRAPHICAL NOTE

CHARLES PEGUY was born in Orléans in 1873. He came of peasant stock and liked to regard himself as coming from the great plain of Beauce, speaking of Chartres as 'my Cathedral'. He was, in fact, brought up by his mother and grandmother in Orléans, and lived all his adult life in Paris. But by heredity, if not by upbringing, he was a peasant, shrewd, obstinate, self-reliant and suspicious, and one can see the image of the Beauce reflected in the slow, flat, repetitive and inevitable rhythm of his writing, just as Orléans fired his imagination and made Joan of Arc the central figure in his work, his patron Saint.

With the help of a scholarship he was sent to the College Louis-le-Grand where he formed the friendships that survived to the end: Lotte, the Tharaud brothers and Baudouin whose sister he married. But when he proceeded to the Ecole Normale, where he came under the influence of Bergson, his independence began to assert itself. He found the severe discipline and the pressure of the educational system irksome and formed a life-long dislike of the 'intellectuals' whose specialised outlook and lack of humanity he rejected. His time and energy were given to the cause of Dreyfus and to a prose drama *Jeanne d'Arc;* then in 1897 he married and with his wife's dowry founded a small publishing business. As a result of all these activities he failed to pass his final examination.

When the funds of the publishing house were exhausted, Lucien Herr, the librarian of the Sorbonne, Léon Blum (the future minister) and three leading Socialists, came to his rescue. But rather than accept their doctrines and their authority, Péguy went his own way and founded *Les Cahiers de la Quinzaine* in which all his own works were to appear and which only survived owing to his capacity for virile begging and the success of some of his friends whose books he published: Romain Rolland, the Tharauds and an occasional volume by Jaurès. But his independence cut him off from the Socialists as completely as it did from the Conservative parties and he was never out of financial difficulties as long as he lived.

Péguy's integrity is the most striking characteristic of his work and the source of his power of integration. It won him friends and led him into an endless series of quarrels on their behalf. His gift for divining motives, a combative spirit and a point of view which few of his contemporaries could fathom did not help to smooth his path. His last 'campaign' was fought on behalf of

BIOGRAPHICAL NOTE

Bergson, whose work was about to be placed on the Index, though this did not prevent his accusing Bergson of failing to support him.

Péguy's private life was overshadowed by difficulties from the moment he returned to the Church which he had left at College. His respect for his wife's freedom prevented him from influencing her in any way, so that their civil marriage was never regularised by the Church nor their children baptised. He remained technically on the threshold of the Church, and the term 'porche' which occurs in the second of the *Mysteries* must have had a special significance for him, in the same way that the theme of 'The Holy Innocents' attracted him partly because the liturgy accepts the unbaptised Jewish children as saints.

Péguy was called up in August 1914 and was killed on the first day of the battle of the Marne.

For many months he had felt that no future lay before his generation and wrote of the fatigue of bearing at one and the same time the miseries of peace and the burdens of war. Yet he held the current belief that the ordeal would be a final one: 'I go a soldier of the Republic to the last of all wars.' Péguy had always been a patriot, despite the fact that pacifism was more fashionable at that time among French Socialists. He had a strong feeling for the soil and for the intimacy of the relationship which exists between the earth and the people who work it. The idea of French soil, or of any soil, being subject to strangers was abhorrent to him.

There were no eye-witnesses of Péguy's death, since all his section died in the engagement, but certain details which have been recorded of his last day are curiously characteristic. The evening before he died the company halted by a sign-post which read Paris 24 kilometres. Nearby was an old barn, converted into a chapel in which stood a mediaeval statue of the Madonna. During the Revolution it had been hidden in the hay. Péguy spent some time in the chapel. He had been in command of the company but an order that the officer in charge should be mounted reduced him to the ranks, for he could not ride. Reinforcements which arrived the next day to see what had happened to the troops engaged in the counter-attack found a line of infantrymen dead among the turnips. One man lay in advance of the company. An officer noted the expression of peace on his face and read the identity disc: Péguy. It meant nothing to him.

Péguy's life appeared to have ended in failure, though this would never have been his own view. Since his death his works have gradually achieved not only fame but also a wide influence. The dull truths which he wished to voice dully, the flat truths which he wished to voice flatly, the sad truth which could be nothing but sad were found to contain, as M. Halevy says, the potential of time-bombs. His attitude towards disaster and failure; that these were things to be endured and that there was nothing fatal about them; was an inspiration to France in the worst days of the war. Even his personal life has had its echoes. At a time when his son Pierre was ill he undertook a pilgrimage to Chartres. He went alone, walking the whole distance in three days. In 1956 11,000 students made the pilgrimage.

In the last ten years twenty biographies of Péguy have been published. Daniel Rops has probably defined the qualities which his compatriots see in Péguy and of which they feel the need today:

"Believing in an age of unbelief, fair-minded at a time of passion, poor in a rich society, hopeful in a climate of despair, Péguy's whole life illustrates the values of protest and revolt."

CPSIA information can be obtained
at www.ICGtesting.com
Printed in the USA
LVHW082229300921
699195LV00014B/575

9 781532 645853